# 18 PAPER DRONES WITH 9 DIFFERENT DESIGNS
# MAKE AND FLY YOUR OWN
# PAPERDRONE

LET'S MAKE EXCITING PAPER DRONES WITH

AERONAUTICAL ENGINEERING PROFESSOR

## LEE HEE-WOO

President of World Paper Aeroplane
Association and Paper Cultural Foundation

## Author Lee Hee-woo

He graduated from the Air Force Academy and he was in the sky as an F-5 fighter pilot. He I also received a Ph.D. in Aeronautical Engineering from Arizona State University.

After much effort in developing the Air Force's T-50 aeroplane, he was discharged as a brigadier general from the Korean Air Force.

He is currently the CEO of drone manufacturing company KEVA Drone Co. Ltd, a visiting professor at the Korea Aerospace Research Institute, and a director at the Chungnam National University General Military System Research Institute.

Also, as President of the World Paper Aeroplane Association, he has launched the "World Paper Aeroplane Competition for Peaceful Reunion and World Peace".

**Tuva Publishing**
www.tuvapublishing.com

**Address**
Merkez Mah. Cavusbasi Cad. No:71
Cekmekoy - Istanbul 34782 / Turkey
Tel: +9 0216 642 62 62

**Make and Fly Your Own Paper Drone**

**First Print**
2019 / June

**All Global Copyrights Belong To**
Tuva Tekstil ve Yayncilik Ltd.

**Content**
Children

**Writer**
Lee Hee-woo

**Editor in Chief**
Ayhan DEMIRPEHLIVAN

**Project Editor**
Kader DEMIRPEHLIVAN

**Graphic Design**
Jong Ie Nara Design Institute
Omer ALP
Abdullah BAYRAKCI
Zilal ONEL

**ISBN**
978-605-9192-75-0

Licensed Edition of the Work
Paper Drones
Copyright 2019, Jong Ie Nara Co., Ltd.
7F Jong Ie Nara Bldg. 166 Jangchungdan-ro, Jung-gu, Seoul, Korea Zip code #04606, www.jongienara.com
All Rights reserved.

TuvaYayincilik  TuvaPublishing
TuvaYayincilik  TuvaPublishing

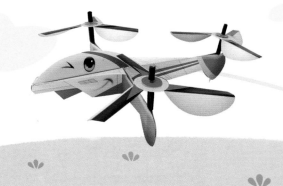

# Introduction

A you work through this book various paper drones will be used as experiential tools for learning science.

One fine autumn day, I was excited to write an unusual book. After putting it off for a long time, I finally brought myself to write a book about paper aeroplanes. Since there were no other books published about paper aeroplanes before, of course I was curious whether anyone would look for it, but fortunately, many young people have found a new interest through this book, and are experiencing a new world of aviation.

Since this book's publication, I have received invitations to lectures and various scientific events. The audiences ranged from kindergarteners to graduate students. It is obvious that paper aeroplanes have been recognised as an excellent tool for young aviators to experimentally access aviation theory through toys that provide children with an interest in flight and science. Thanks to this, I have received the nickname "Paper Plane Doctor".

In 2003, I published *I am the Best Paper Plane Pilot*, which theoretically organised and improved the performance of paper aeroplanes. By classifying paper aeroplanes into 'folded types' and 'assembled types', I made it possible to experience a more diverse paper aeroplane world, as well as making it easier to understand aeronautical theory in a concise and simple way.

Since then, various assembled paper aeroplanes have been developed with more mobility and stability. This is the process that has led us to age of drones. Usually, a 'drone' means a 'multi-copter' with several propellers. However, in actual industrial fields, fixed-wing drones, which are conventional aircraft types, are used much more than this. The reason is that fixed-wing drones have a relatively good flight effectiveness, long flight duration, fast speed, and are stable in windy conditions. With this in mind, this book uses already existing assembled paper planes as the basis to apply a more precise control concept and improved performance to recreate paper drones in the shape of fixed-wing drones, and among the hundreds of paper drones developed in the past, we carefully selected the models with excellent performance and gathered them together to publish *Paper Drone*. Through this book, I hope you use paper drones as experimental tools to learn and experience the science of drones while assembling and enjoying flying the models, which are future leaders of the fourth industrial age.

Lee Hee-woo
Doctor of Aeronautical Engineering,
Arizona State University, USA
President World Paper Aeroplane Association
and Paper Cultural Foundation

No. 1 / Super Glider … Page 28
No. 2 / T-50 … Page 30
No. 3 / F-15 … Page 32
No. 4 / SU-27 … Page 34

# CONTENTS

## Part 1

# About Drones

In TV programmes, drones are often used to film beautiful scenery. Recently, as interest in drones has increased and the industry is booming. The drones are considered to be one of the promising fields in the fourth industrial revolution era, and this reflects the growing trend of industry interest in drones. Let's take a look at the various drones that will change our future.

# About Drones

## What are Drones?

**Drone**
KD-3_KEVA Drone

**Toy Drone**

These days, drones are toys enjoyed by people of all ages, and are also becoming the core of future industries involving media filming, exploration and broadcasting. The dictionary definition of a drone is "an Unmanned Aerial Vehicle System (UAV) which can fly and steer via radio remote control or a pre-programmed course without a person entering the aircraft." However, nowadays the definition of 'drone' is being expanded to include unmanned vehicles such as boats, submersibles, and other vehicles. The origin of the word 'drone' comes from the buzzing or 'droning' sound made by bee drones.

# Drone Types and History

Drones can be classified generally into three types of aircraft. The first type is a fixed-wing drone that flies like a standard aeroplane. Then there is the rotary type which uses several motors to maintain level flight (similar to a helicopter or multi-coptor). Lastly there is the VTOL (Vertical Take-Off & Landing) type which uses both rotors and fixed wings. The history of fixed-wing drones goes back to the 1910s, when the First World War was in full swing.

In 1913, American aviation engineer Lawrence Sperry created an autopilot flight system using a gyroscope (a device used to measure and maintain the orientation of a spinning top, regardless of its rotation in any direction), and electrical engineer Charles Kettering used this to create the "Kettering Bug", an unmanned aircraft which was named after him.

This plane was designed as a self-destructing UAV, intended to be loaded with explosives and aimed at the enemy, however it was not used, because the war ended, and remained in history as the world's first drone.

Rotary drones have come to be the most representative drone type, since the appearance of the first multi-coptor.

The AR drone, which was presented at the 2010 International Electronics Fair (CES) in Las Vegas, USA, was produced by PARROT, a French toy car manufacturer, and was the first of its kind. The AR drone is a small aircraft of 57cm in size, but it can be taken off and landed vertically as soon as it is removed from the box and it can also be controlled using a mobile phone, which gained considerable media interest and saw a boom in the drone market.

According to the UAV Dictionary, published in the US, drones are used for over 300 commercial purposes, including broadcasting. The use of drones is expected to continue to increase, combined with technological development and business ideas.

**Fixed-Wing Drone**
Same design as an aeroplane

**Kettering Bug**

Developed in 1918
The world's first drone

**AR Drone**

Developed by Parrot
Modern drone

**Broadcast Drone**
Typical for commercial use
A drone with a camera
attached

# Drone Uses

Drones have long been used for military purposes, but it wasn't until recently the drone boom has really picked up speed. It's due to the fact that drones have become so close to everday life as the parts became smaller and more refined with IT development.

While in the past drones could only be flown at altitudes of 500m or higher, with the appearance of smaller drones equipped with precise flight control devices, they were finally able to fly at lower than 500m altitudes, which has brought about a revolutionary change. One of the uses of drones for industrial purposes, not for military purposes, is an agricultural unmanned helicopter for the Japanese Yamaha Motor Corporation.

Drones have since become widely used for such purposes as surveying, filming and broadcasting, lifesaving, pipeline and cable inspection, wildlife observation, and delivering relief goods to disaster-hit areas.

There are different uses for the fixed-wing drones and the rotary-wing drones mentioned above. Fixed-wing drones are somewhat inconvenient compared to multi-copters with vertical take-off and landing because they require a certain

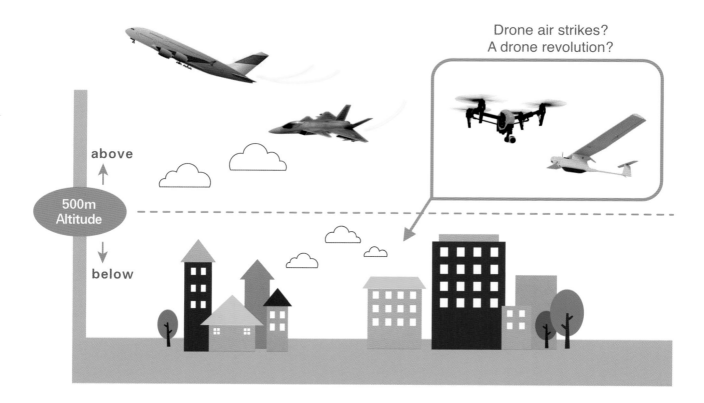

distance to take off and land. However, they have excellent flight efficiency, can undertake long-term flight, they are fast, and are strong against wind. Thus, fixed-wing drones have advantages in exploring large areas or operating over the ocean. On the other hand, the rotary-wing drones are difficult to fly for a long time due to low flying efficiency, slower flight speed, and they are more susceptible to wind. However, because they can take off and land vertically and are relatively easy to control, they can be used for various purposes in relatively limited space.

Let's look at the types of drones: fixed-wing drones, rotary-wing drones, and VTOL drones.

## Fixed-Wing Drone

Fixed-wing drones are structurally identical to general aeroplanes, so they are often used for military field and industrial facility inspection, border surveillance, ship surveillance, fishing and communication relay. They use engines, props, etc., to gain momentum and the wing is able to gain lift. So, just as aeroplanes need runways, fixed-wing drones also need a lot of space. Because they need to maintain a constant speed to stay in the air at a particular altitude, it is easy to see that they cannot hover or fly at low speeds.

## Rotary-Wing Drone

Rotary-wing drones fly on a lift that is provided by the propeller. These drones are categorised into quadcopters, hexacopters, octocopters, etc, depending on how many propellors they have. Compared to fixed-wing drones, their flight efficiency and speed, as well as altitude are not so impressive, but they are still widely used.

They can fly in any direction, so they are often used in various industries and leisure fields requiring short-distance flying, such as search and rescue, forest fire monitoring, small goods delivery and filming.

## VTOL (Vertical Take Off and Landing) Drone

VTOL drones can take off or land vertically without a runway and they also have a similar cruising speed range as a normal aeroplane. They have both the advantages of fixed-wing drones capable of high-speed long-haul flights and the advantages of rotary wing drones capable of vertical takeoff and landing. They are mainly used as military fighters or as futuristic weapons.

 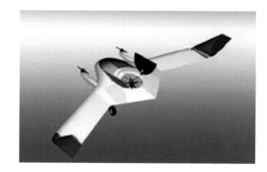

# The Birth of Paper Drones

In general, when people think of drones, they think of multi-copter type drones.

But for industrial applications, fixed-wing drones are used much more than multi-copters (a type of rotary-wing drone which flies using two or more rotating wings).

This is because fixed-wing drones are superior to multi-copters in terms of flight efficiency, and relatively superior in terms of speed, running time and economy.

So, this book adds to the concept of flying paper aeroplanes by introducing them in the form of fixed-wing paper drones. Usually a paper aeroplane is a kind of glider, flying by purely throwing force without the concept of control.

However paper drones use the power of elastic bands to manipulate the flight surfaces to perform various types of manoeuvre. In other words, this book describes paper aeroplanes that can be controlled as paper drones.

In addition, paper drones are not made of foldable paper aeroplanes, but are made of prefabricated construction materials using rigidly designed paper, so that they can be manufactured in a shape similar to a real aircraft, and can be sophisticated in manoeuvering.

These paper drones were born as an opportunity to use paper aeroplanes to experimentally identify aerodynamic phenomena while studying aeronautical engineering in the past.

In other words, when I was a combat pilot, I had a curiosity that if I attached a control surface to a paper aeroplanes, it would not be a simple glider, but I could also do a lot of experiments and create a pilotable aeroplanes capable of flying acrobatics.

Part 3, Paper Drone Assembly Process, contains several paper drone designs that I have developed over the past 20 years with excellent manaeuverability and stability.

Fly your paper drone just like a pilot!

# Aircraft Development History

**1452** — Leonardo Da Vinci (1452-1529) dreamed of flying like a bird and did a lot of research.

**1783** — On December 1, Sharur and Rovay succeeded in raising a balloon 8.58m in diameter.

**1903** — Americans, the Wright brothers, succeeded in making the first gasoline powered aircraft. It flew 36m on the first test, 59m on the second, 66m on the third and 260m on the fourth test for 59 seconds. Flyer No. 1 (USA)

**1909** — Louis Blériot succeeded in crossing the 38km distance between Britain and France for the first time in the world. Blériot XI (France)

**1916** — During the First World War, several excellent aeroplanes appeared. Out of these, the SPAD S.VII was considered one of the best. SPAD S.VII (France)

**1939** — Dr. Ernst Heinkel of Germany developed the world's first jet. It is one of the models that Hitler allowed for practical use. Heinkel He178 (Germany)

**1940** — The first helicopter was put into practical use. It had one rotating wing and three auxiliary wings on the tail. Sikorsky VS-300 (USA)

**1945** — At the end of World War II, the United States began making great efforts to develop the jet aircraft. This started the history of the fighter jet. Lockheed P-80 Shooting Star (USA)

**1947** — The American Chuck Yeager became the first pilot to break the sound barrier, ushering in the era of supersonic flight. Bell XS-1 (USA)

**1969** — The era of mass transport by aircraft began. Development began in the 1960s, and the representative model is the Boeing 747. Boeing 747 (USA)

**1989** — Stealth aircraft were developed with concealment techniques designed to evade detection systems, including opponents' radar, infrared, acoustic and visual detection. F-117 (USA)

SUPER GLIDER

## Part 2

# Principles of Flight

In order to experience the new world of Paper Drones, it is important to understand the principles of flight listed here.

Let's make paper drones with the best performance by referring to the assembly instructions.

When you perform a test flight according to the methods presented here, you will find yourself in a world of paper drones that you never knew before.

# Flight Principles of Paper Drones

## Paper Drones and Aerodynamics

Is the principle of flying a paper aeroplane different from an actual aeroplane?

Actually, it isn't. Among things that fly through our skies, there are bees and butterflies smaller than paper aeroplane, and jumbo jets which are much bigger.

They may be very different in size, but the principles of flight are the same. Therefore, paper aeroplanes are an excellent material to learn about and enjoy the principles of flight at your fingertips.

## Four Kinds of Forces Acting on an Aeroplane

All flying objects in the sky have the following four forces acting on them.

① Lift: The force that causes the aeroplane to overcome gravity and float into the sky, occurring on the wings of an aeroplane.

② Gravity: The force exterted by the Earth pulling objects down (gravity).

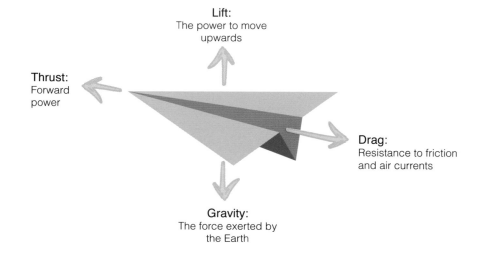

Lift:
The power to move upwards

Thrust:
Forward power

Drag:
Resistance to friction and air currents

Gravity:
The force exerted by the Earth

③ Drag: The force acting on the an aeroplane's surface in the direction opposite to the direction of travel of the vehicle due to the friction and aerodynamic resistance of the air.

④ Thrust: The power generated from the engine, overcoming drag and pushing the vehicle forwards.

Since paper drones have no engine, thrust means the force of the throwing hand or pulling force. When the above four forces are balanced, the aeroplane flies at a constant speed.

If the lift is greater than gravity, it will fly upwards, and the speed will increase when the thrust is greater than drag.

# The Principle of Generating Lift

The principle of lift generation can be experienced in a very simple experiment.

As shown in the picture, when you blow on the top side of the paper, the paper receives a force which pushes it upward. The secret of this power is the principle of the generation of lift.

The Principle of Generating Lift

In other words, if the air flow on the upper side of the paper becomes faster than the lower side, the pressure acting on the upper surface becomes lower than the lower surface and the pressure difference on the upper and lower surfaces of the paper results in the lift force, which is called Bernoulli's theorem. Let's apply this principle to the wing to learn the principle of generation of lift. The cross section of the wing is generally flat on the underside and round on the top.

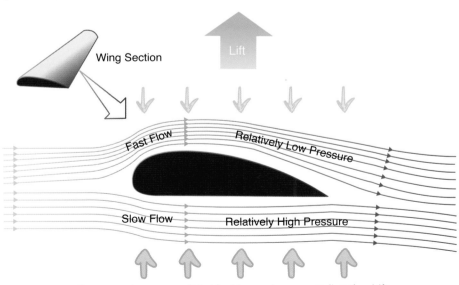

Wing Section

Lift

Fast Flow

Relatively Low Pressure

Slow Flow

Relatively High Pressure

Downward pressure (High) - Upward pressure (Low) = Lift

## ✈ Bernoulli 🏁

In 1738, Daniel Bernoulli, a Swiss physicist, quantified the relationship between flow velocity and pressure in his book, *Hydrodynamica*. He tested the speed of water in glass tubes of different thicknesses, observing that the water flowing through the thinner glass tubes increased in speed while the speed of the water flowing through the thicker glass tubes decreased. Thus, he published Bernoulli's theorem, which states that pressure increases as fluid velocity increases and pressure decreases as fluid velocity decreases.

When these wing sections are exposed to an air flow, two air streams hit the wing, one on the upper surface of the wing, one on the lower surface of the wing and then meet again at the wing end.

At this time, the air particles flowing across the upper surface of the wing flow faster than the air particles flowing across the lower surface at the same time, and the pressure difference occurs on the upper and lower surfaces of the wing due to Bernoulli's theorem. This is 'Lift'.

The shape of the wing cross-section is slightly different depending on the aeroplane. The wing cross-section of low-speed aircraft is thick, while the wing cross-section of high-speed aircraft is thin.

In the case of paper drones, there is no thickness to the blade section, but it has a slight bent shape as shown in the figure bellow, and lift occurs by the same principle. The magnitude of the lift generated on the wing depends on the shape of the blade section, and on the relative angle with respect to the air flow (angle of attack).

In other words, as the angle of attack increases, the lift increases proportionately, and the drag also increases proportionately. However, when the angle of attack exceeds a certain level, the drag increases rapidly and the lift is reduced.

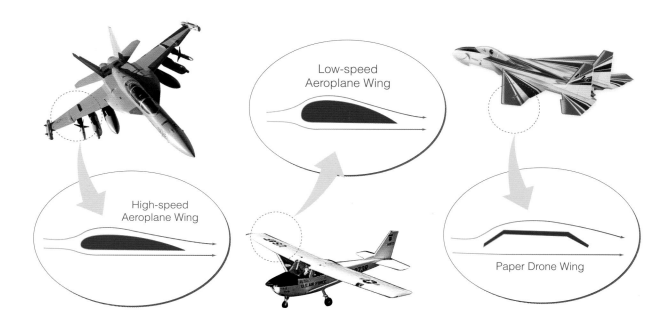

Low-speed Aeroplane Wing

High-speed Aeroplane Wing

Paper Drone Wing

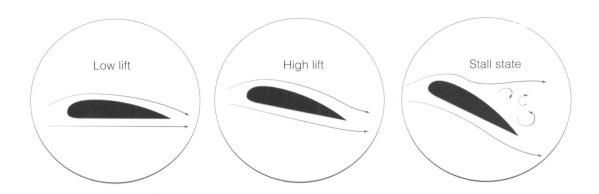

Low lift   High lift   Stall state

This is called a "stall". Stalling causes aircraft crashes.

As you ride in a car, let your hand out through the window and feel the pressure of the air on your palm. This feeling helps us understand how the lift on the wing varies with the wind direction.

The cause of the stall is that when the angle of attack is above a certain level, the air that has contacted the upper surface of the wing section can no longer flow along the surface of the wing but is deflected instead. All aeroplanes with fixed wings have a lowest possible flight speed, because below the minimum speed the wing's angle of attack exceeds a certain level causing the aeroplanes to stall and fall. A device used for the purpose of delaying or preventing such stalls is referred to as a 'high-lift device'. High-lift devices serve to prevent stalling and maximise lift under low-speed flight conditions, such as aircraft take-off and landing. Flaps and slats are typical examples of this.

## Flaps

The flap is attached to the back of the main wing of the aircraft to increase the area of the wing and the angle of attack to obtain additional lift. This device is mainly used only at take-off and landing because the drag increases simultaneously.

## Slats

The slat has the same function as the flap, but it is mounted in front of the main wing and increases the lift by increasing the camber on the wing.

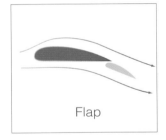

Flap

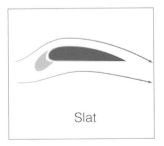

Slat

※Flaps and slats are also used in paper drones because they have the effect of increasing the strength of the wings, in addition to the lift increase effect.

# The Principle of Controlling an Aeroplane

In addition to basic operations such as ascending, descending, and turning, an aircraft can perform all kinds of acrobatic flights in a three-dimensional space by pilot manipulation.

To do this, the control device used by the pilot is connected to the control surface attached to the outside of the aeroplane and the movement of the control surface changes the aeroplane's posture.

Typical maneuvering surfaces include the 'elevator' on the horizontal tail wing, the 'rudder' on the vertical tail wing and 'ailerons' on the left and right ends of the wings.

If you implement these control functions in paper drones, you can create controllable paper drones, which is the biggest feature and advantage you can get from this book.

The following figures illustrate the name and location of the control surfaces used on paper drones when fully assembled. It is important to understand these, as they are frequently used terms in the paper drones production process. Next, let's see how these control surfaces play a role in aircraft control.

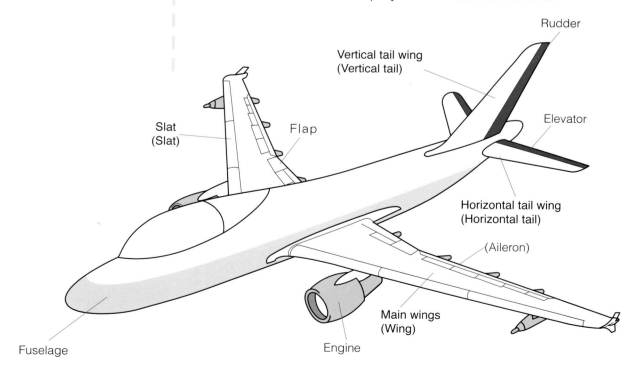

Rudder

Vertical tail wing (Vertical tail)

Slat (Slat)

Flap

Elevator

Horizontal tail wing (Horizontal tail)

(Aileron)

Main wings (Wing)

Fuselage

Engine

① **Elevator:** The moment generated by the elevator adjusts the aeroplane into an ascending or descending posture. This process is known as pitching.

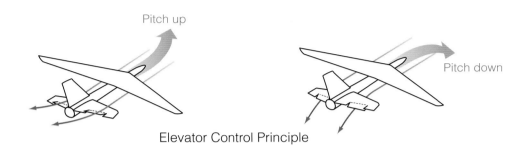

Elevator Control Principle

② **Rudder:** The moment generated by the rudder adjusts the aeroplane into an left-or right-turning posture. This movement is called yawing.

Rudder Control Principle

③ **Aileron:** The aeroplane posture is inclined to the left and right due to the lift difference between the left and right wings generated by moving in opposite directions. This movement is called rolling.

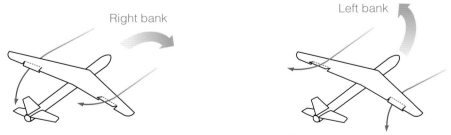

Aileron Steering Principle

To raise or lower an aeroplane, the pilot uses the elevator. When turning to the left or right, the rudder and the aileron are used simultaneously.

# Test Flight

## I'm a Test Pilot too

A test flight pilot is a veteran class pilot who tests and evaluates newly developed aeroplanes after completing a test pilot flight course. Test flight is a crucial step that determines the success or failure of the flight development process and usually takes more than 1,000 sorties (sortie: one single flight of an aircraft). For the paper drones you make, you have the authority and qualification as a test flight pilot. The paper drones will vary greatly in performance when they first fly and after flight modifications. In addition, this test flight and modification work will give you a lot of understanding and skill regarding flight.

## Launch Tips

How you launch a paper drone is very important. However well you make it, if the launch method is incorrect, the drone cannot show off its full potential.

When holding a paper drone for launch, it is best to hold it as near to its centre of gravity as possible. When throwing a paper drone, it is best to hold it slightly above shoulder height and throw it by pushing it forward, with the feeling of pushing and letting go rather than throwing.

Also, with paper drones, it is important to check the symmetry of the airframe and the angle of the wings, flaps, and ailerons. This is equivalent to a pilot checking the flight condition before each flight in case of an actual aeroplane.

Throw in a straight line

# Horizontal Straight Flight (Trim Control)

The first stage of the test flight is to adjust the control surfaces and body of the aeroplane so that the aeroplane has a gentle and constant inclination angle and flies straight and horizontally. Controlling an aeroplane is the act of making the aircraft fly in the desired direction by moving the control surface connected to the controls. Here, control surfaces are the rudder and elevators, attached to the rear wing, and the ailerons on both main wings.

## Elevator Control

The elevator is a manoeuvering plane that allows the aircraft to fly at the required angle of inclination.

① If you dive after ascending, reduce the angle of the elevator.
② If the flight distance is short, the angle of the elevator should be increased.
③ Normal flight.

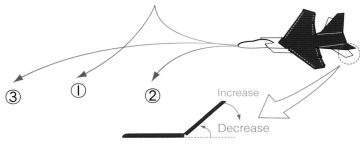

Flight Angle and Control

## Aileron Control

The aileron is the control surface that makes the aeroplane bank left and right, And it can be used to prevent tilting during flight.

① If the aeroplane tilts to the left, lower the left aileron and raise the right aileron.
② If the aeroplane tilts to the right, lower the right aileron and raise the left aileron.

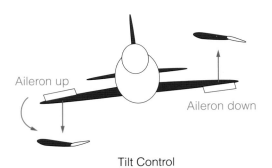

Tilt Control

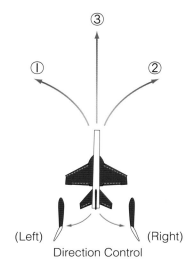

(Left)    (Right)

Direction Control

## Rudder Control

The rudder does not need to be adjusted if the structure of the aeroplane is normal, but if aileron adjustment does not eliminate the tilting, use the rudder.

① If the aeroplane tilts to the left, move the tail rudder to the right.

② If the aeroplane tilts to the right, move the tail rudder to the left.

③ Normal flight.

# Aerobatics

If the test flight achieves stable level flight, it means that the aeroplane is complete. The next stage is aerobatics.

For aerobatic flight, sufficient thrust is required, so use a rubber-band launch method. Enough space is required for aerobatics, so a room with a high ceiling, such as a gymnasium is appropriate.

1 rubber band

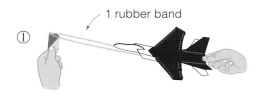

2 rubber band

Rubber Band Launch Tips

## Starting a Loop

The loop is one of the most visible maneuvers at an air show, drawing a circle vertically. In order to perform the loop start, the angle of the elevator should be slightly increased before launch. The radius of the loop depends on the angle of the elevator.

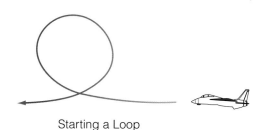

Starting a Loop

## Aileron Roll

Another popular air show stunt, involves rolling the aeroplane horizontally while flying straight forward. To perform an aileron roll, adjust the left and right ailerons counterclockwise and launch.

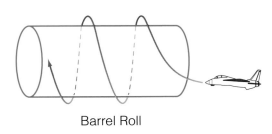

Aileron Roll

## Barrel Roll

A barrel roll is a kind of manoeuvre that draws a spiral flight trajectory as the aeroplane progresses. In order to perform a barrel roll, it is necessary to increase the angle of the elevators slightly after the control surfaces are set the same as for an aileron roll.

Barrel Roll

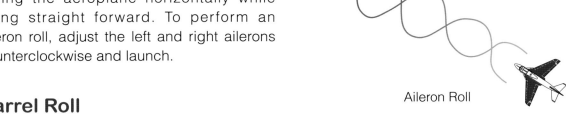

# Republic of Korea Air Force

## Special Flight Team (Black Eagles)

*Black Eagles*

On September 25, 1995, the Black Eagles, a professional aerobatic flight team from the Air Force 8th Fighter Wing, was officially launched to great public attention. Since then, the Air Force has been contributing to the progress of globalisation of the Air Force and bringing the Air Force closer to the people.

Aerobatic flight is a stunning flight performance that dramatically changes the posture and altitude of an aeroplane to decorate its flight trajectory in a visually pleasing or impressive way. It is more difficult than ordinary flying, requires strong physical strength and intense concentration to withstand the G-force, which can be up to 4-5 times a person's bodyweight, and expert teamwork, and requires perfect aircraft maintenance.

The Black Eagles are comprised of six A-37 aircraft, and these A-37s are called Dragonflies. It is a two-seater aircraft with a length of about 9 metres, a wing width of about 12 metres, a height of 3 metres, a cruising speed of 250 knots, maximum speed of 750 km/h (Mach: 0.7) and a range of 200 miles. The interval between manoeuvres can be minimised, allowing for continuous manoeuvres within a small area. It is also suitable for special flight because it has good stability and thrust as well as excellent flight characteristics such as lift to propulsion ratio, a low stall speed and two engines.

# Transition of the Korean Air Force

**1920** .............. 
Beginning

### JN-4D Training Aeroplane
The training aeroplane used at the Korean Flight School in The Willows, California, founded in 1920.

**1949** .............. 
Establishment

### L-4 Liaison Plane
Acquired 20 liaison aircraft from the US Army and established the ROKAF. The first aircraft of the ROKAF.

**1950** ..............

### T-6 Founding Plane
A two-seater trainer introduced on the 14th May, 1950, as a donation from the people upon the founding of the Republic of Korea.

**1950** .............. 
June 25

### F-51 Fighter
The first fighter plane of the ROKAF.

**1951** ..............

### O-1A Observer
A two-seat observer aeroplane introduced during the Korean War, it was responsible for reconnaissance and operational communications. Until 1961, it was used for elementary flight training to train pilots.

**1955** ..............

### F-86 Fighter
The first jet fighter to be introduced in accordance with the Air Force's plan to increase its power.

**1965** ..............

### F-5A Fighter(Freedom Fighter)
The Air Force's first supersonic fighter.

**1969** ..............

### F-4D Fighter-bomber
A multi-purpose combat bomber.

**1986** ..............

### F-16 Fighter
A fighter equipped with state-of-the-art equipment.

**2003** ..............

### T-50 Advanced Training Plane
The first advanced trainer developed in Korea.

**2005** ..............

### F-15K
Korea's main fighter aeroplane.

## Part 3

# Paper Drone
# Assembly Process

# 🔩 No. 1 Super Glider

The albatross is the bird that can fly the longest, and it can fly several tens of kilometers by gliding alone. This No. 1 is a glider that takes advantage of the Albatross' flight characteristics, and it has high stability and long-term flight capability, though its mobility is low. It is simple and easy to manufacture and it is suitable as Paper Drone No. 1. Also, since the aeroplane only has an elevator, it is suitable as an entry-level stage to experience the piloting of paper drones.

## Test Flight

The Super Glider can fly for a long time with its long wings and light airframe. In addition, since its centre of gravity is at the bottom, its roll stability is superior compared to other models.

The super glider has one vertical tail wing and may tilt to the left or right if this is not straight. In this case, check the drone from the front to see if the tail is bent. If it still tilts, adjust the rudder to correct the tilt.

# Super Glider

## Assembly Tips  ·Design Paper: Pages 49-52, Pages 85-88

- To prevent twisting of the fuselage, it is recommended to keep the book dry and use a thick bookmark. (Prevention of fuselage twisting is very important for flight performance after completion.)
- After assembling, give a slight vertical angle to both wings to help roll stability.
- The pasted part should be dried enough (at least 10 minutes) to maintain the centre of gravity and rigidity.

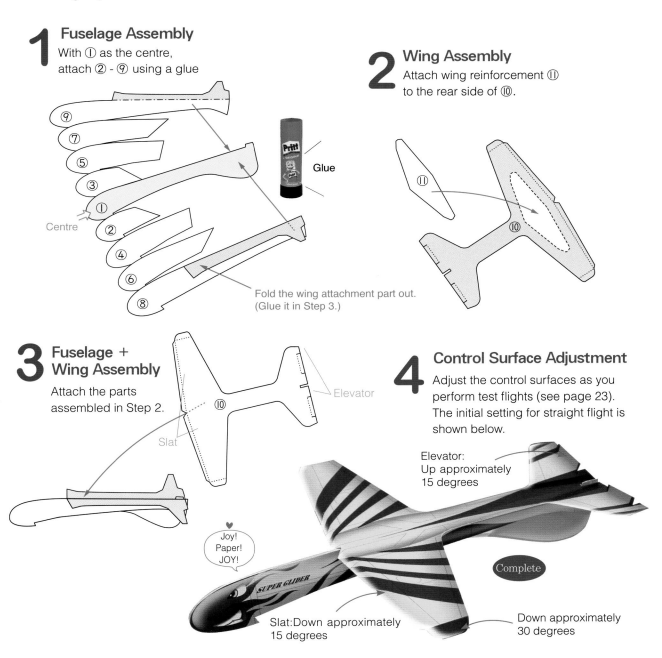

**1 Fuselage Assembly**
With ① as the centre, attach ② - ⑨ using a glue

Centre

Glue

Fold the wing attachment part out.
(Glue it in Step 3.)

**2 Wing Assembly**
Attach wing reinforcement ⑪ to the rear side of ⑩.

**3 Fuselage + Wing Assembly**
Attach the parts assembled in Step 2.

Elevator

Slat

Joy!
Paper!
JOY!

**4 Control Surface Adjustment**
Adjust the control surfaces as you perform test flights (see page 23). The initial setting for straight flight is shown below.

Elevator:
Up approximately
15 degrees

Complete

SUPER GLIDER

Slat:Down approximately
15 degrees

Down approximately
30 degrees

## No. 2 T-50 (Golden Eagle)

As part of an ambitious plan to acquire a next-generation advanced training aeroplane to assist in the training of elite pilots in the 2000s, the T-50 (Advanced Trainer) was developed in 1993 through international cooperation between Korea Aerospace Industries Co. Ltd. and Lockheed Martin. Compared to other aircraft in its class, it has a wide main wing and a high thrust-to-weight ratio of close to 1.0, and high vertical turning performance. It is also equipped with advanced avionics equiment such as HUD (Heads-Up Display) and MFD (Multi-Function Display) in order to make it easy for pilots to adapt to next generation high-performance fighters such as the F-16 or higher. It is equipped with a turbofan engine to ensure economic efficiency as a trainer and it has been exported to four countries because of its armed capability, and is attracting attention in the light fighter aircraft and advanced trainer aircraft markets.

## Test Flight

The T-50 has one vertical tail wing and may tilt to the left or right if this is not straight. In this case, check the drone from the front to see if the tail is bent. If it still tilts, adjust the rudder to correct the tilt. The T-50 is also suitable for enjoying various aerobatic flights using the control surfaces because of its light weight.

# T-50 (Golden Eagle)

## Assembly Tips  ·Design Paper: Pages 57-60, Pages 93-96

- To prevent twisting of the fuselage, it is recommended to keep the book dry and use a thick bookmark. (Prevention of fuselage twisting is very important for flight performance after completion.)
- Adjusting the aileron to an appropriate angle also contributes to an increase in wing lift and maintenance of the strength of the wing.
- After assembly, the pasted part should be dried enough (at least 10 minutes) to maintain the centre of gravity and rigidity.

## 1 Fuselage Assembly

With ① as the centre, attach ② - ⑦ using a glue.

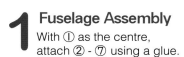

## 2 Wing Assembly

Attach wing reinforcement ⑨ to the rear side of ⑧.

Fold the wing attachment part out.
(Glue it in Step 3)

## 3 Fuselage + Wing Assembly

Attach the parts assembled in Step 2.

Elevator

Slat

Aileron

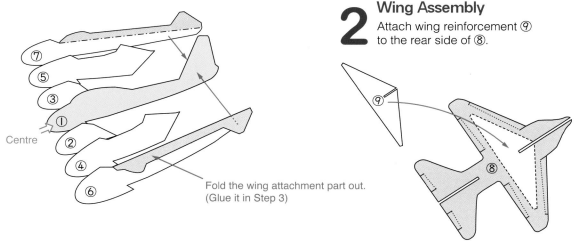

## 4 Control Surface Adjustment

Adjust the control surfaces as you perform test flights (see page 23). The initial setting for straight flight is shown below.

Elevator:
Up approximately 15 degrees

Slat:
Down approximately 15 degrees

Aileron:
Down approximately 15 degrees

Joy!
Paper!
JOY!

Complete

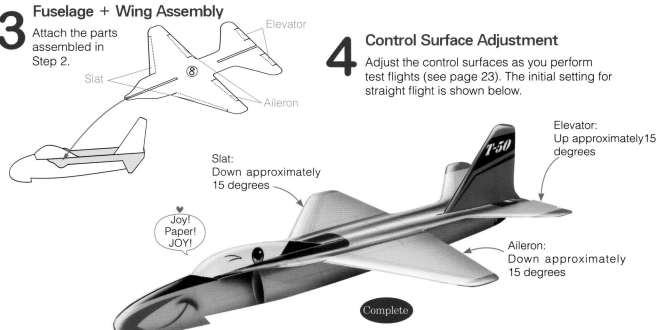

# ⚙️ No. 3 F-15 (Eagle)

The US Air Force felt the need for new fighters to take control of the Vietnam War. It was also stimulated by the development MIG-25s, capable of more than Mach 2, in the Soviet Union. So US Air Force adopted the F-15 as proposed by McDonnell Douglas at the time in 1969. The F-15 has a wing shape with a 38 degree retraction angle and the engine inlet is designed to be adjustable to automatically adjust the air inflow to the optimum depending on the flight speed and altitude. The F-15 was rated as one of the top fighters in the world after presenting overwhelming dominance in the Battle of Bekaa Valley in 1979 and the more recent Gulf War, engaging with MIG-21s, 23s, and 25s. There are several variants of the F-15, including A/B and C/D superiority variants, both of which serve in air-to-air combat roles, and the E variant, which has excellent ground attack capability. The F-15K is an improved version of E, reborn as a multi-purpose fighter and is currently used as the main fighter of the Korean Air Force.

## Test Flight 🛩️

Since the F-15 has two vertical tail wings, its directional stability is good. In addition, because of its excellent stability, it is a model that can be enjoyed not only through hand throwing but also acrobatic flight using a rubber band launch. You can also learn the effect and control principle of each control surface (aileron, elevator, rudder, slats) by using them in a similar way to that of an actual aeroplane.

# F-15 (Eagle) • • • • • • • • • • • • • • • • • • • • • •

## Assembly Tips  ·Design Paper: Pages 57-60, Pages 93-96

- Be careful not to bend the fuselage while assembling it and let it dry thoroughly (at least 10 minutes) before flying it.
- Attach both vertical tail wings exactly parallel to the fuselage direction.
- The nose section may spread due to impact shocks, so be sure to glue it firmly.
- Adjusting the aileron to an appropriate angle also contributes to an increase in wing lift and maintenance of the strength of the wing.

**1 Fuselage Assembly**
With ① as the centre, attach ② - ⑦ using a glue.

**2 Wing Assembly**
Attach wing reinforcement ⑨ to the rear side of ⑧. Fold ⑩ and ⑪ in half.

Centre

Fold the wing attachment part out.
(Glue it in Step 3.)

**3 Fuselage + Wing Assembly**
Attach ⑩ and ⑪ to the ◆ shapes on (8), and then attach ⑧ to the fuselage.

Slat
Elevator
Aileron

**4 Control Surface Adjustment**
Adjust the control surfaces as you perform test flights (see page 23). The initial setting for straight flight is shown below.

Slat:
Down approximately 15 degrees

Joy! Paper! JOY!

Elevator:
Up approximately 15 degrees

Aileron:
Down approximately 15 degrees

Complete

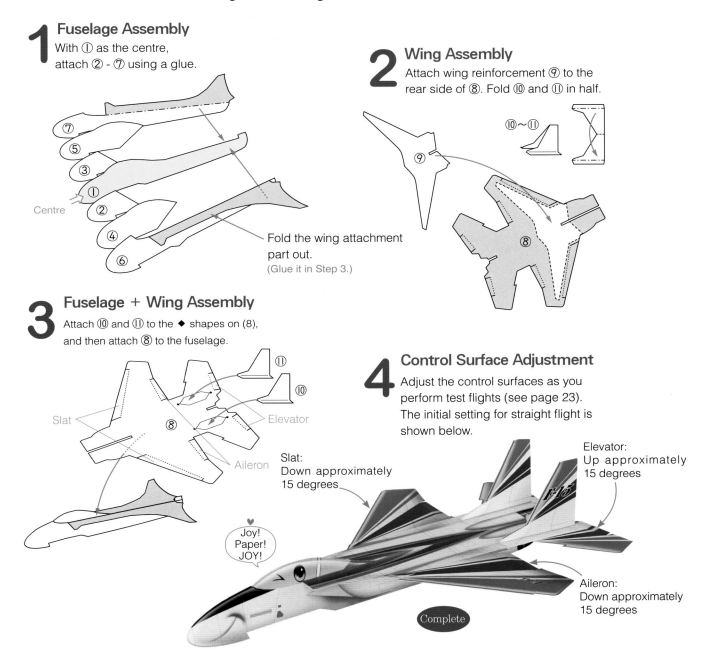

# No. 4 SU-27

The SU-27 was a long-range interceptor designed to counter the US F-15 by the Soviet Union and was deployed in 1985 after a long development period. This aircraft is known as a mysterious fighter capable of manoeuvering hooks and cobra moves that cannot be mimicked by other fighters, in addition to its long-range capability. However, its aviation electronics and armed operations are significantly inferior to the F-15. The SU-27 was rebuilt as the best fighter in Russia, upgraded to the SU-35, with modernised weapon systems when flying towards the ground, which had previously been pointed out as a disadvantage of the SU-27.

## Test Flight

Since the SU-27 has two vertical tail wings, its directional stability is good. Also, because the wings are large and the turning radius is short, it is an excellent aircraft with diverse aerobatic performance. The flight performance using the control surfaces is similar to the F-15. The SU-27 is more appropriate for rubber band launching than hand throwing, and you can also learn the effect and control principle of each control surface (aileron, elevator, rudder, slats) by using them in a similar way to that of an actual aeroplane.

# SU-27

## Assembly Tips  ·Design Paper: Pages 61-64, Pages 97-100

- Be careful not to bend the fuselage while assembling it and let it dry thoroughly (at least 10 minutes) before flying it.
- The nose section may spread due to impact shocks, so be sure to glue it firmly.
- Attach both vertical tail wings exactly parallel to the fuselage direction.
- Adjusting the aileron to an appropriate angle also contributes to an increase in wing lift and maintenance of the strength of the wing.

**1 Fuselage Assembly**
With ① as the centre, attach ② - ⑦ using a glue.

**2 Wing Assembly**
Attach wing reinforcement ⑨ to the rear side of ⑧.
Fold ⑩ and ⑪ in half.

**3 Fuselage + Wing Assembly**
Attach ⑩ and ⑪ to the ◆ shapes on ⑧, and then attach ⑧ to the fuselage.

**4 Control Surface Adjustment**
Adjust the control surfaces as you perform test flights (see page 23). The initial setting for straight flight is shown below.

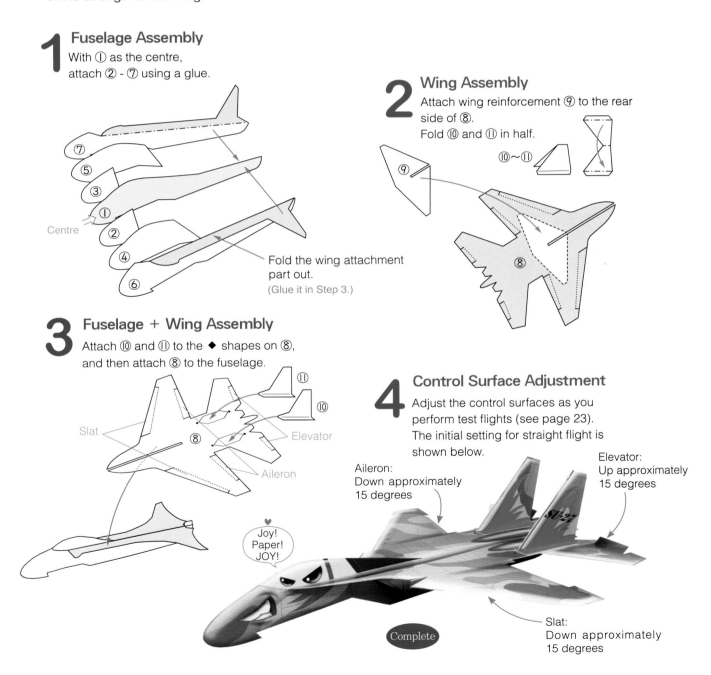

Centre

Fold the wing attachment part out.
(Glue it in Step 3.)

Slat

Elevator

Aileron

Joy! Paper! JOY!

Aileron:
Down approximately 15 degrees

Elevator:
Up approximately 15 degrees

Slat:
Down approximately 15 degrees

Complete

# No. 5 F-18 (Hornet)

The F-18 was developed to replace the US Navy's F-4 and Marines' A-7 as a multipurpose combat aircraft for both air and ground attacks, complementing the US Navy's flagship F-14. The F-14 is a powerful carrier-capable fighter (which is loaded onto a warship) however, it was very expensive, which led the manufacturer to develop the F-18 in 1975, based on Northrop's YF-17. The long strake of the wing, which is a special external feature of the F-18, increases the lift of the main wing when the nose is raised (high angle of attack) and serves to reduce the wave drag during supersonic flight. There are approximately 900 F-18s currently operating with the US Navy, and Canada, Spain, and Australian Air Forces.

## Test Flight

Since the F-18 has two vertical tail wings, its directional stability is good. It is more appropriate for rubber band launching than hand throwing, and you can also learn the effect and control principle of each control surface (aileron, elevator, rudder, slats) by using them in a similar way to that of an actual aeroplane. The F-18 has excellent manoeuvrability, and it is strong enough for a variety of acrobatic flights using the rubber band launch method.

# F-18 (Hornet) ● ● ● ● ● ● ● ● ● ● ● ● ● ● ● ● ● ● ● ● ● ● ● ● ● ● ● ●

## Assembly Tips ·Design Paper: Pages 65-68, Pages 101-104

● Be careful not to bend the fuselage while assembling it and let it dry thoroughly (at least 10 minutes) before flying it.

● The nose section may spread due to impact shocks, so be sure to glue it firmly.

● Attach both vertical tail wings exactly parallel to the fuselage direction.

● Adjusting the aileron to an appropriate angle also contributes to an increase in wing lift and maintenance of the strength of the wing.

**1** **Fuselage Assembly**
With ① as the centre, attach ② - ⑦ using a glue.

**2** **Wing Assembly**
Attach wing reinforcement ⑨ to the rear side of ⑧. Fold ⑩ and ⑪ in half.

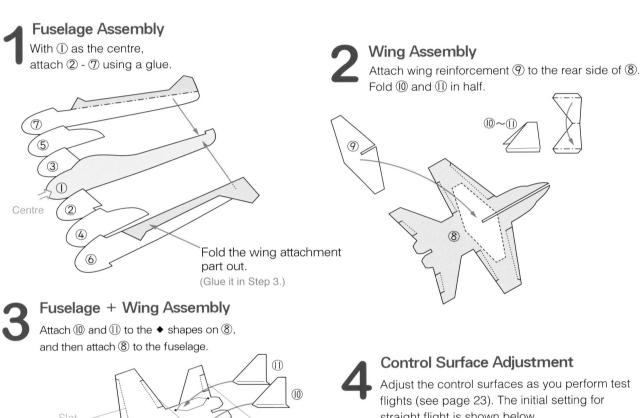

Centre

Fold the wing attachment part out.
(Glue it in Step 3.)

⑩～⑪

**3** **Fuselage + Wing Assembly**
Attach ⑩ and ⑪ to the ◆ shapes on ⑧, and then attach ⑧ to the fuselage.

**4** **Control Surface Adjustment**
Adjust the control surfaces as you perform test flights (see page 23). The initial setting for straight flight is shown below.

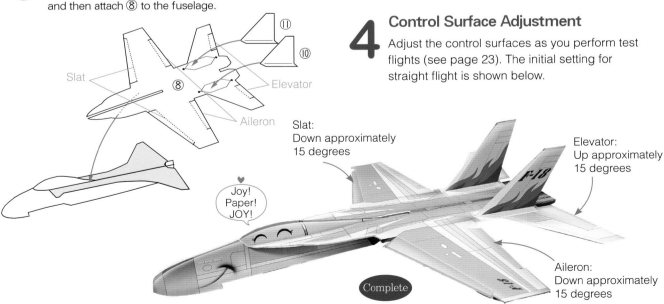

Slat

Elevator

Aileron

Joy! Paper! JOY!

Slat:
Down approximately 15 degrees

Elevator:
Up approximately 15 degrees

Aileron:
Down approximately 15 degrees

Complete

## No. 6 Harrier

The Harrier is the main fighter of the British Navy, a vertical takeoff and landing fighter-bomber designed to fly from an aircraft carrier and support ground forces. The Harrier, which was co-developed by the United Kingdom and the United States, first flew in 1966. It can operate in narrow areas such as naval ships because it can take off and land vertically although it does have the disadvantage of being relatively less armed. The Harrier is not equipped with the same machine guns as other fighter jets because it is less able to perform vertical take off or landing when armed with bombs or missiles. The Maritime Harrier was put into battle in the British Falkland Islands in 1982 and achieved an impressive record in battle against the Argentine Air Force.

## Test Flight

The Harrier has one vertical tail wing and may tilt to the left or right if this is not straight. In this case, check the drone from the front to see if the tail is bent. If it still tilts, adjust the rudder to correct the tilt. Since the Harrier has a relatively long fuselage, it has excellent horizontal flight; pitch stability and directional stability, and since it has a tough body, it is very suitable for rubber band launching.

# Harrier ·················

## Assembly Tips  ·Design Paper: Pages 69-72, Pages 105-108

- Be careful not to bend the fuselage while assembling it and let it dry thoroughly (at least 10 minutes) before flying it.
- The nose section may spread due to impact shocks, so be sure to glue it firmly.
- Be sure to glue the two engine intake sections firmly on either side.
- Adjusting the aileron to an appropriate angle also contributes to an increase in wing lift and maintenance of the strength of the wing.

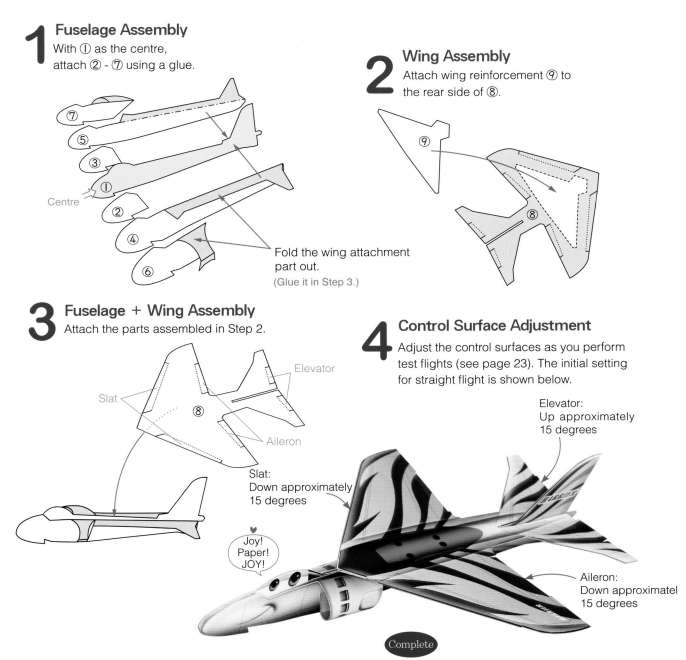

**1 Fuselage Assembly**
With ① as the centre, attach ② - ⑦ using a glue.

Centre

Fold the wing attachment part out.
(Glue it in Step 3.)

**2 Wing Assembly**
Attach wing reinforcement ⑨ to the rear side of ⑧.

**3 Fuselage + Wing Assembly**
Attach the parts assembled in Step 2.

Elevator
Slat
Aileron

Slat:
Down approximately
15 degrees

Joy!
Paper!
JOY!

**4 Control Surface Adjustment**
Adjust the control surfaces as you perform test flights (see page 23). The initial setting for straight flight is shown below.

Elevator:
Up approximately
15 degrees

Aileron:
Down approximatel
15 degrees

Complete

# No. 7 F-22 (Raptor)

The F-22 was developed as part of the US Air Force's enhancement project, replacing the F-15, the world's best known fighter. The fighter was developed as the first radar-invisible stealth aircraft in the world and is also known as the world's most expensive aeroplane with advanced technology such as artificial intelligence. In particular, the F-22 is capable of supersonic flight up to Mach 1.5 without the use of an afterburner, making it far superior in flight capability. The F-22 is one of the world's powerful fighters, with no other fighter able to match it one-on-one.

## Test Flight

Since the F-22 has two vertical tail wings, its directional stability is good. The F-22 is more appropriate for rubber band launching than hand throwing, and you can also learn the effect and control principle of each control surface (aileron, elevator, rudder, slats) by using them in a similar way to that of an actual aeroplane. The F-22 has excellent manoeuvrability, and it is strong enough for a variety of acrobatic flights using the rubber band launch method.

# F-22 (Raptor) • • • • • • • • • • • • • • • • • • • • •

## Assembly Tips  ·Design Paper: Pages 73-76, Pages 109-112

● Be careful not to bend the fuselage while assembling it and let it dry thoroughly (at least 10 minutes) before flying it.

● The nose section may spread due to impact shocks, so be sure to glue it firmly.

● Attach both vertical tail wings exactly parallel to the fuselage direction.

● Adjusting the aileron to an appropriate angle also contributes to an increase in wing lift and maintenance of the strength of the wing.

**1 Fuselage Assembly**
With ① as the centre,
attach ② - ⑦ using a glue.

⑦
⑤
③
①
Centre
②
④
⑥

Fold the wing attachment part out.
(Glue it in Step 3.)

**2 Wing Assembly**
Attach wing reinforcement ⑨ to the rear side of ⑧.
Fold ⑩ and ⑪ in half.

⑩~⑪

⑨
⑧

**3 Fuselage + Wing Assembly**
Attach ⑩ and ⑪ to the ◆ shapes on ⑧,
and then attach ⑧ to the fuselage.

⑩
⑪
Slat
⑧
Elevator
Aileron

**4 Control Surface Adjustment**
Adjust the control surfaces as you perform test flights (see page 23). The initial setting for straight flight is shown below.

Aileron:
Down approximately
15 degrees

Elevator:
Up approximately
15 degrees

Joy!
Paper!
JOY!

Complete

Slat: Down approximately
15 degrees

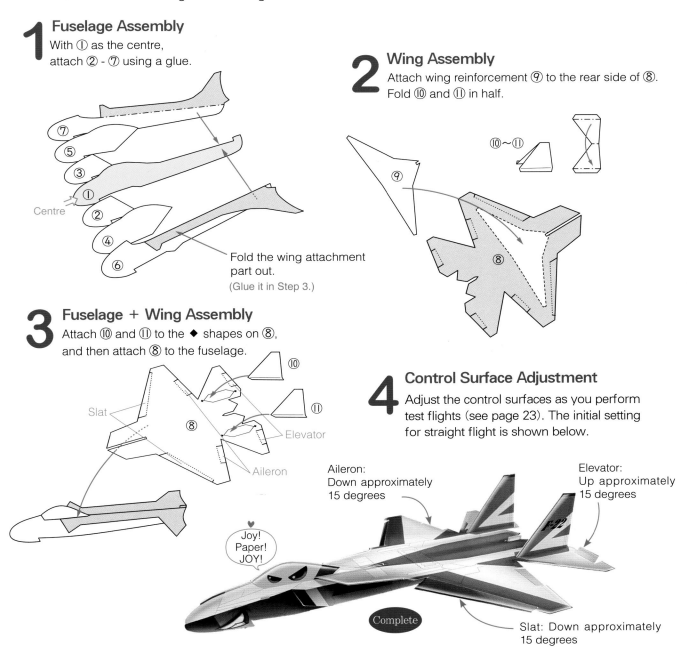

## 🛠 No. 8 Black Eagle

The Black Eagle was developed to replace the A-37, an airshow aircraft for the Korean Air Force, with the T-50 variant modified for air shows. Compared to other aircraft in its class, it has a wide main wing and a high thrust-to-weight ratio of close to 1.0 and it has excellent turning performance and vertical manoeuverability. In 2015, it made its first appearance at the World Air Show in England and had the honour of winning the trophy.

## Test Flight 🛩

The Black Eagle has one vertical tail wing and may tilt to the left or right if this is not straight. In this case, check the drone from the front to see if the tail is bent. If it still tilts, adjust the rudder to correct the tilt. The Black Eagle is also suitable for enjoying various aerobatic flights using the control surfaces because of its light weight.

# Black Eagle ● ● ● ● ● ● ● ● ● ● ● ● ● ● ● ● ●

## Assembly Tips  ·Design Paper: Pages 77-80, Pages 113-116

● To prevent twisting of the fuselage, it is recommended to keep the book dry and use a thick bookmark. (Prevention of fuselage twisting is very important for flight performance after completion.)

● Adjusting the aileron to an appropriate angle also contributes to an increase in wing lift and maintenance of the strength of the wing.

● After assembly, the pasted part should be dried enough (at least 10 minutes) to maintain the centre of gravity and rigidity.

### 1 Fuselage Assembly
With ① as the centre, attach ② - ⑦ using a glue.

### 2 Wing Assembly
Attach wing reinforcement ⑨ to the rear side of ⑧.

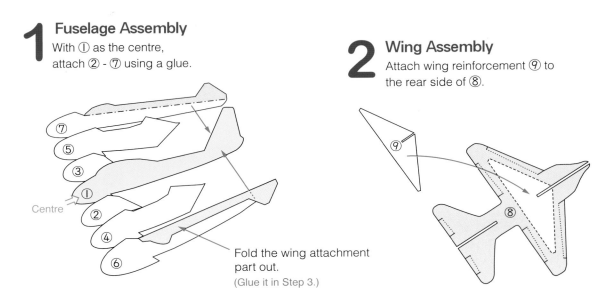

Centre

Fold the wing attachment part out.
(Glue it in Step 3.)

### 3 Fuselage + Wing Assembly
Attach the parts assembled in Step 2.

Elevator

Slat

⑧

Aileron

### 4 Control Surface Adjustment
Adjust the control surfaces as you perform test flights (see page 23). The initial setting for straight flight is shown below.

Joy! Paper! JOY!

Slat:
Down approximately 15 degrees

Elevator:
Up approximately 15 degrees

Aileron:
Down approximately 15 degrees

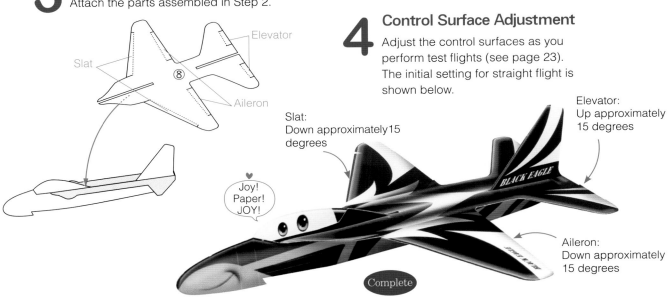

Complete

# 🔧 No. 9 VTOL Drone "Joy"

VTOL (Vertical Take Off and Landing) means taking off and landing by moving vertically rather than forward. It is technically difficult to solve the shortcomings of helicopters in horizontal flight, and those of aeroplanes which need long runways to take off and land, and to gain the advantages of both. It was over 10 years since the first test flights in 1953 before this became possible, however it is now being researched in more detail. Here, it has been given the name Joy, and as you slowly assemble it from the diagrams, you may find yourself exclaiming "Joy, paper joy!"as you let your dreams fly into the world of the future.

'Joy' is an old Korean pronunciation of the word for paper, and in English 'joy' means a feeling of happiness and enjoyment. When you finish making your paper drone, how about shouting 'Joy!' out loud?

## Test Flight ✈

The VTOL is centre-weighted because the main wing is upright and the propeller is horizontal, so is not suitable for horizontal straight flight. When you drop it gently from a height, you can see its rotor turn as it flies downward.

# VTOL Drone "Joy" • • • • • • • • • • • • • • •

## Assembly Tips ·Design Paper: Pages 81-84, Pages 117-120

● To prevent twisting of the fuselage, it is recommended to use clips after assembly. (Prevention of fuselage twisting is very important for flight performance after completion.)

● When assembling the fuselage, assemble the centre part first, insert a toothpick, and stick the toothpick in so that it does not shake.

● After assembly, the pasted part should be dried enough (at least 10 minutes) to maintain the centre of gravity and rigidity.

### 1 Fuselage Assembly 1
Stick ⑥ and ⑦ together using a glue, and then put the assembled part through the central hole in ①.

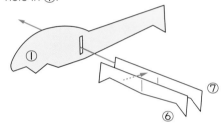

### 2 Fuselage Assembly 2
Attach parts ② to ⑤ to Fuselage Assembly ① in order.

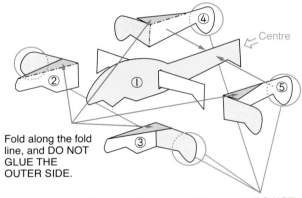

⟵ Centre

Fold along the fold line, and DO NOT GLUE THE OUTER SIDE.

Check the "completed" picture and DO NOT apply glue to the areas where the propellers will be attached. The propellers should be attached last.

### 3 Propeller Assembly
Mount ⑧ to ⑪ on a toothpick. (Glue ⑨ and ⑩ together, but do not use glue on ⑧ or ⑪.)

⑧    ⑨       ⑩    ⑪

Toothpick.

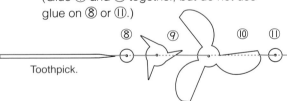

Wind and attach ⑫ around the toothpick above and below the attached propeller. (To attach ⑫ best, first wind it around the toothpick once, then unwind and add glue to fix it in place.)

### 4 Control Surface Adjustment
Attach the propellers to the fuselage and check that the propellers spin when the drone is dropped gently from a high place.

Joy! Paper! JOY!

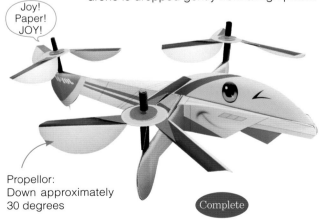

Propellor: Down approximately 30 degrees

Complete

# Things Every Paper Aeroplane Pilot Should Know

# Making a Launch Pad and How to Fly

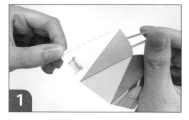

**1** Hook the rubber band on the round hole and pull it inwards.
(※ Launcher design paper is on pages 49-120 with every aeroplane design.)

**2** Apply the glue to the white side of the paper and fold along the fold lines.

**3** Use your thumb to grip the rubber band and pull it tight.

**4** If using one rubber band is too short, you may attach a second.

**5** Hook your paper drone to the rubber band on the launcher, pull it back, and launch your drone with power.

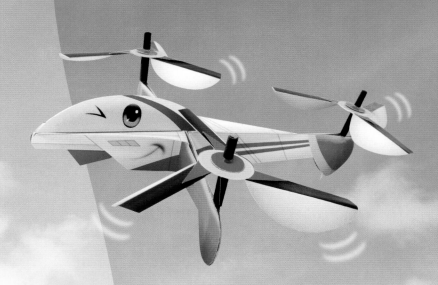

# Part 4

# Paper Drone
# Design Paper

# Aviation Journal
## Paper Drone Log Book

Pilot Name: _____

### Paper Drone Pilot Pre-flight Inspections and Cautions for Best Flight

- For the safety of others, fly during the daytime and not at night.
- Check the drone's left/right wing balance both before and after every flight.
- Check the adjustment amount of the paper drone's wings and control surfaces.
- When flying outside, check the wind direction and fly in the same direction as the wind is blowing.
- Adjust the elevator and rudder according to the paper drone's glide condition.
- Do not throw paper drones toward people or animals.
- The pilot should fly in as open a space as possible in order to maintain eye contact with the paper drone.
- Do not fly paper drones in public or crowded places.

| Date | Paper Drone Name | Flight Location | Farthest Flight Distance | Longest Flight Time | Notes |
|------|------------------|-----------------|--------------------------|---------------------|-------|
|      |                  |                 |                          |                     |       |
|      |                  |                 |                          |                     |       |
|      |                  |                 |                          |                     |       |
|      |                  |                 |                          |                     |       |
|      |                  |                 |                          |                     |       |
|      |                  |                 |                          |                     |       |
|      |                  |                 |                          |                     |       |
|      |                  |                 |                          |                     |       |
|      |                  |                 |                          |                     |       |
|      |                  |                 |                          |                     |       |
|      |                  |                 |                          |                     |       |
|      |                  |                 |                          |                     |       |
|      |                  |                 |                          |                     |       |
|      |                  |                 |                          |                     |       |

Drone pilots record the drone's flight status, crew names, aircraft condition, etc.
When flying your paper drones, you can also record where you fly them, how far they fly,
how long they stay in the air, what time you flew them, etc.!

**Super Glider**

·Remove along the lines and assemble according to the guide on page 29.

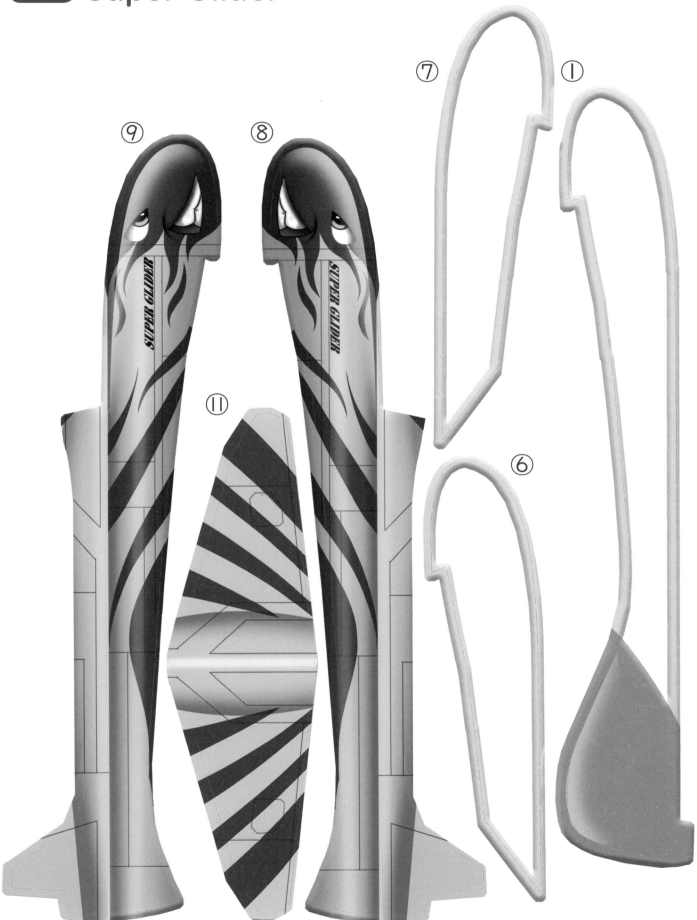

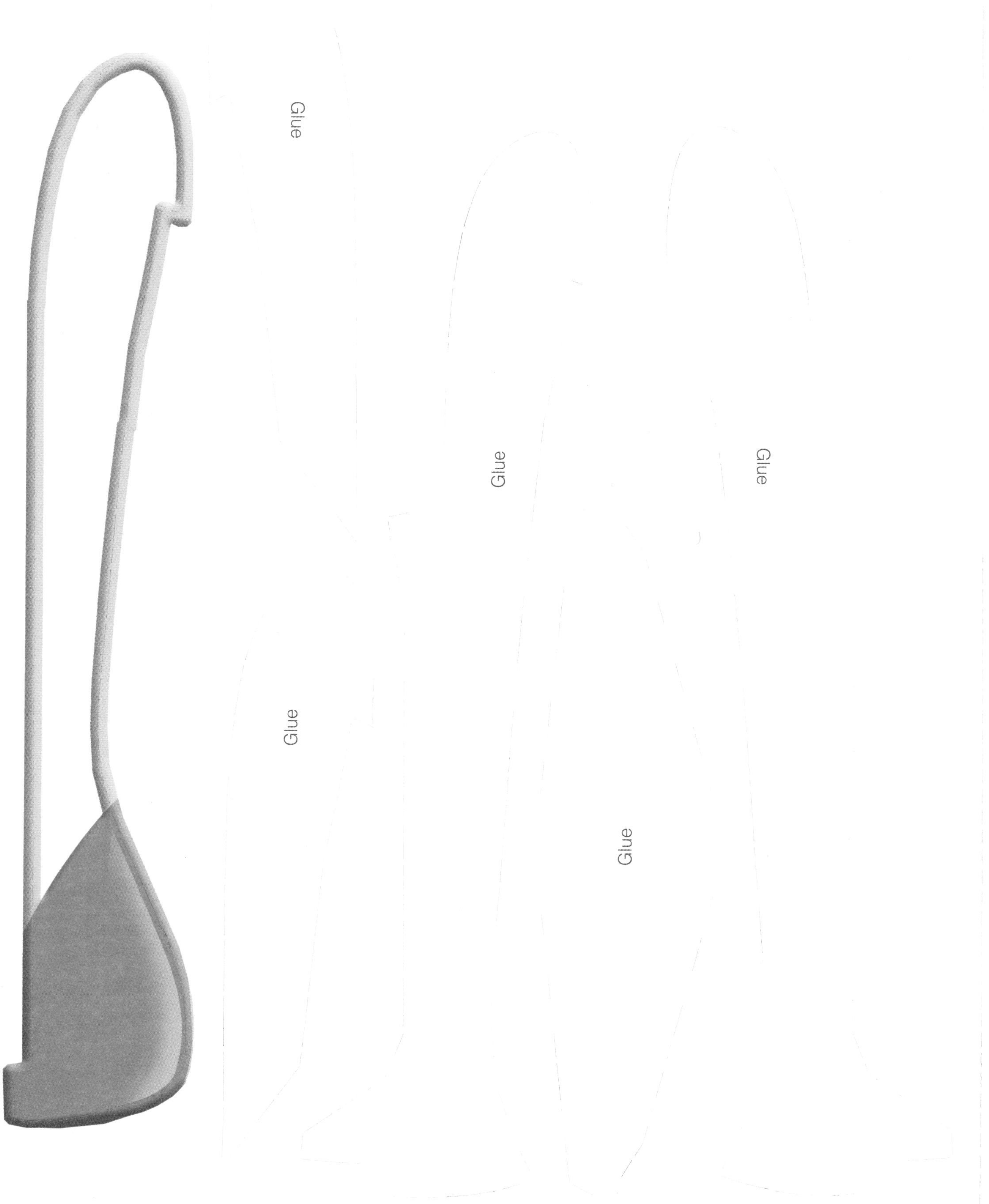

Glue

Glue

Glue

Glue

Glue

**Super Glider**

·Remove along the lines and assemble
according to the guide on page 29.

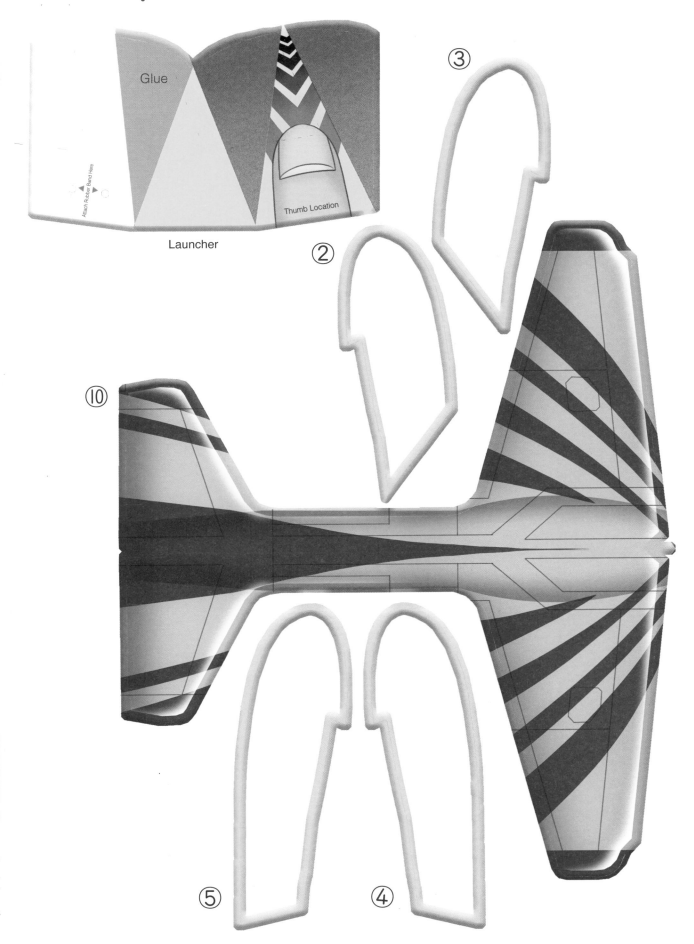

Glue

Attach Rubber Band Here

Thumb Location

Launcher

③

②

⑩

⑤

④

Please pull out along the

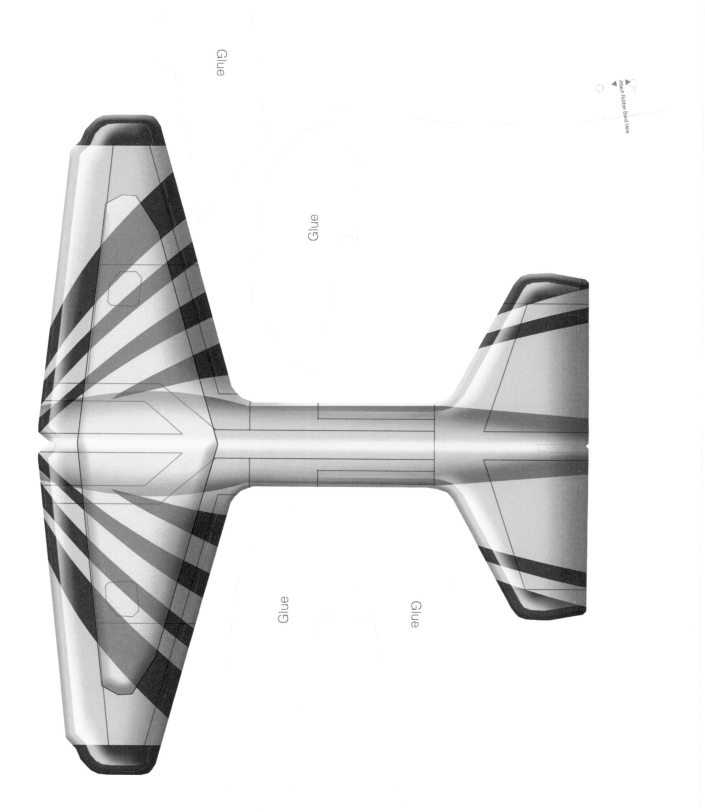

Glue

Glue

Glue

Glue

Attach Rubber Band Here

·Remove along the lines and assemble according to the guide on page 31.

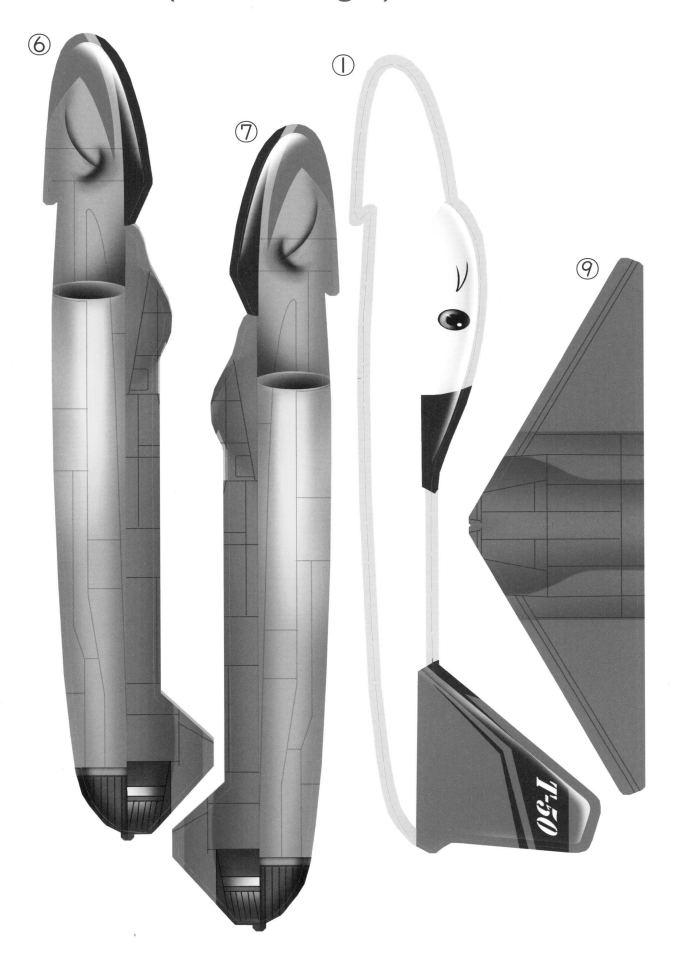

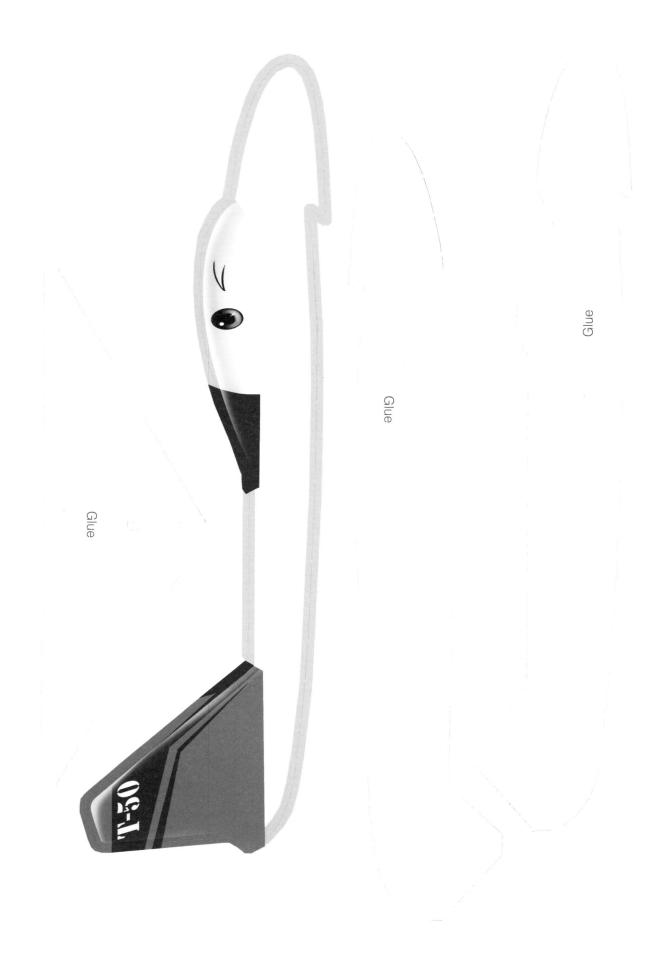

Glue

Glue

Glue

T-50

# No. 2 T-50 (Golden Eagle)

·Remove along the lines and assemble according to the guide on page 31.

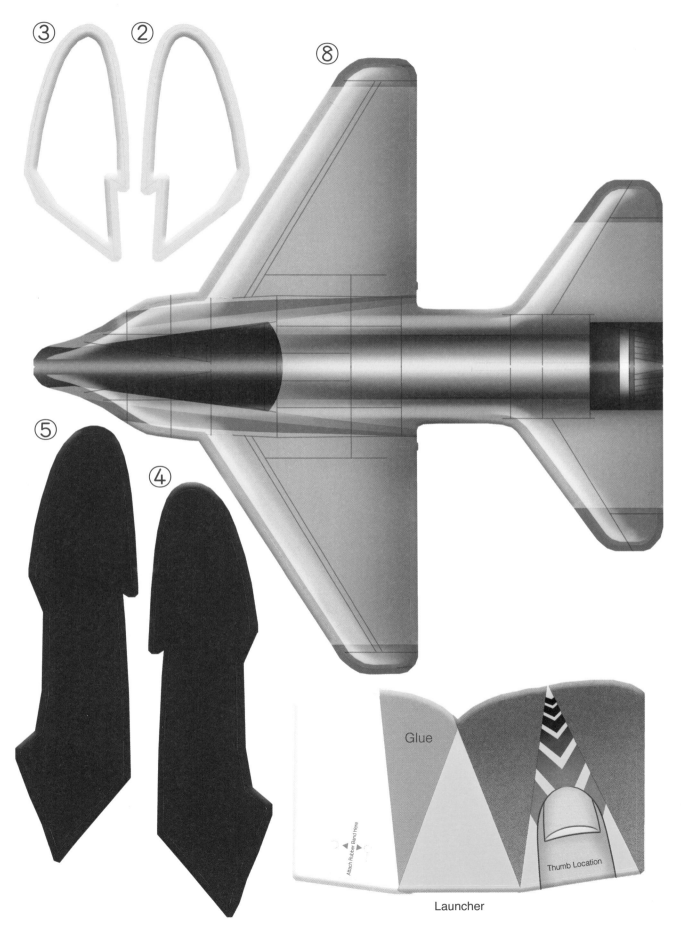

Glue

Attach Rubber Band Here

Thumb Location

Launcher

55

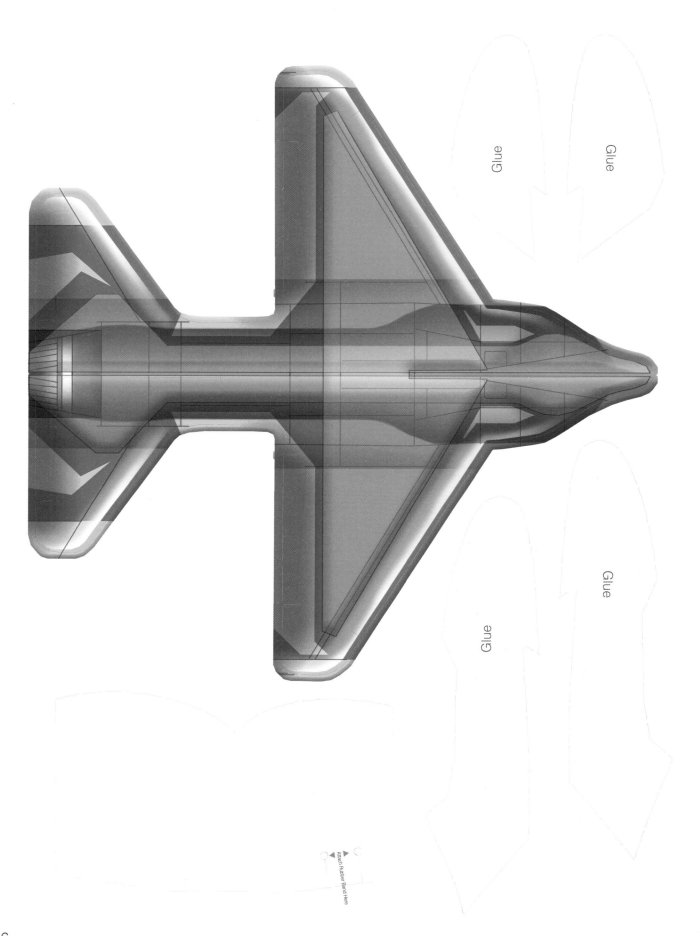

Glue

Glue

Glue

Glue

Attach Rubber Band Here

# No. 3 F-15 (Eagle)

·Remove along the lines and assemble according to the guide on page 33.

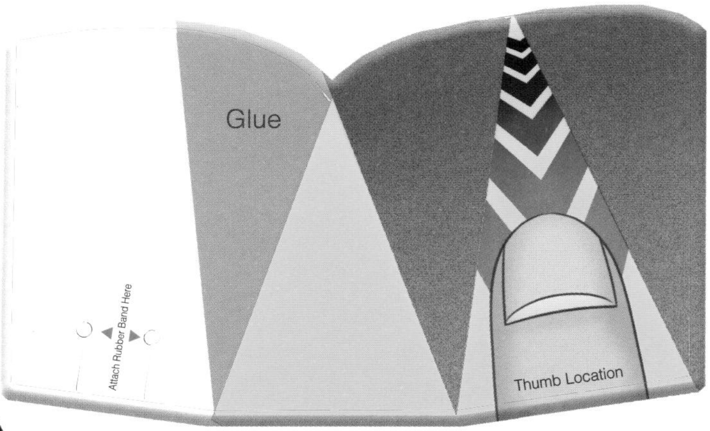

Glue
Attach Rubber Band Here
Thumb Location

Launcher

⑥

⑨

⑦

①

Please pull out along the

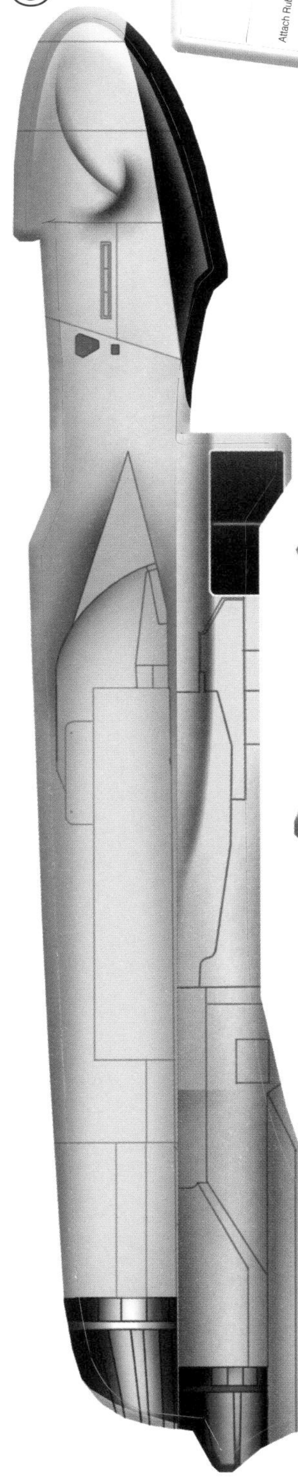

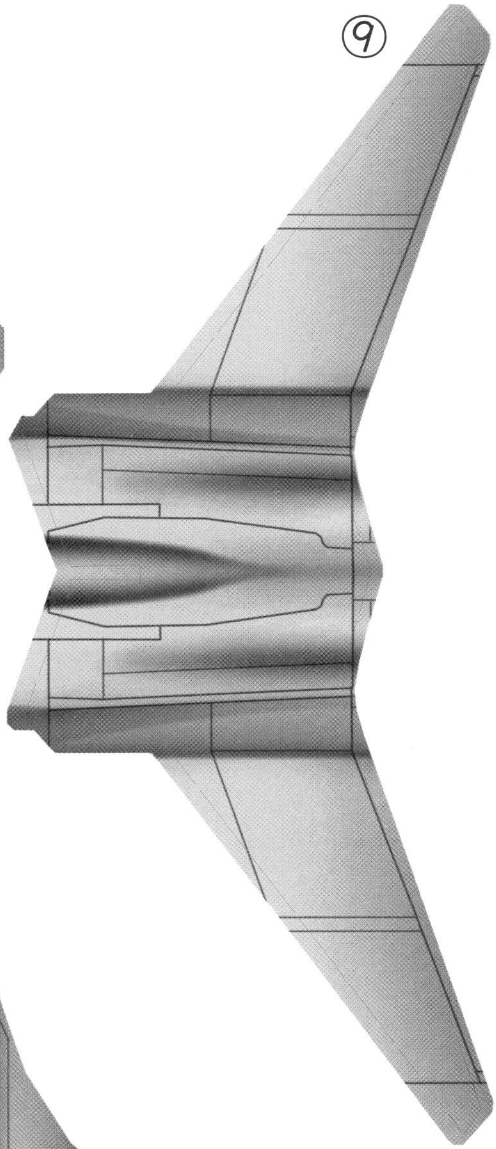

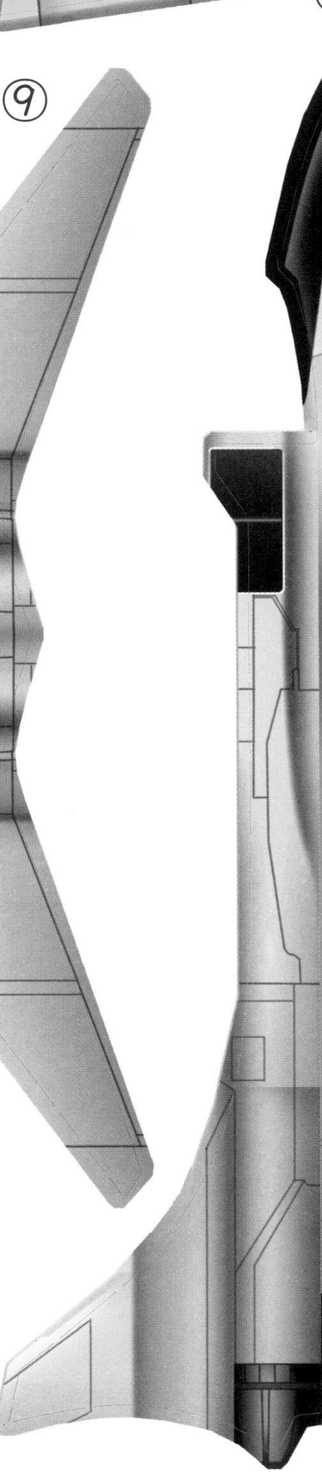

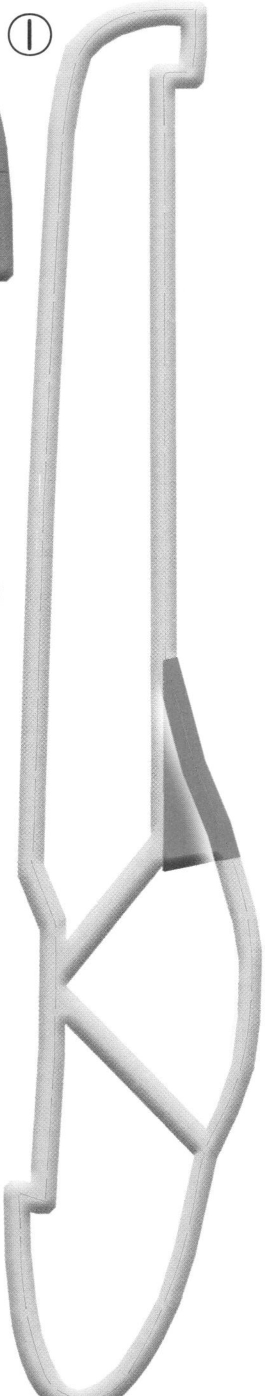

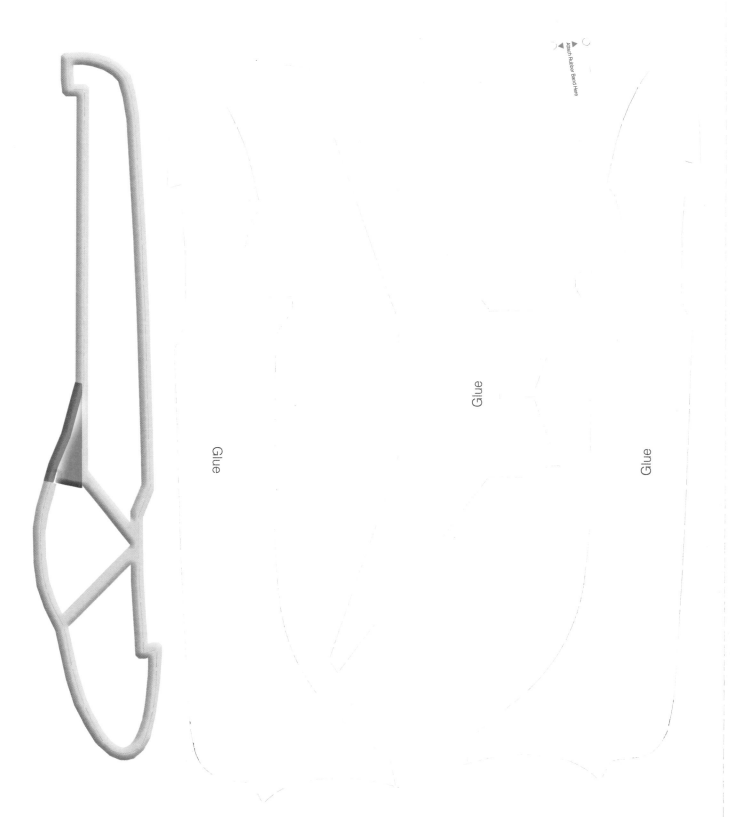

Glue

Glue

Glue

Attach Rubber Band Here

**No. 3** F-15 (Eagle)

·Remove along the lines and assemble
according to the guide on page 33.

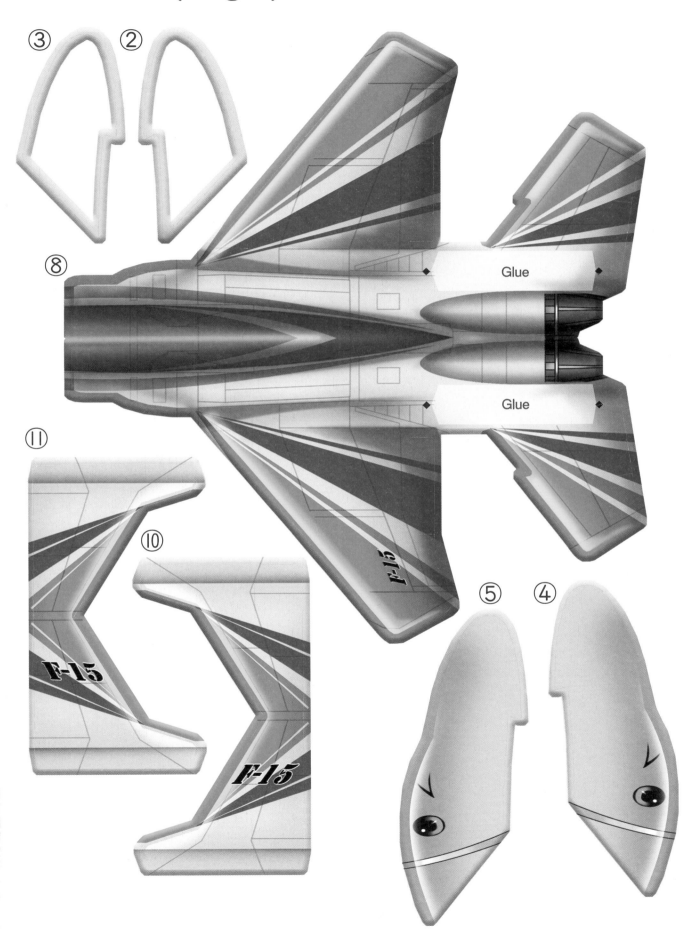

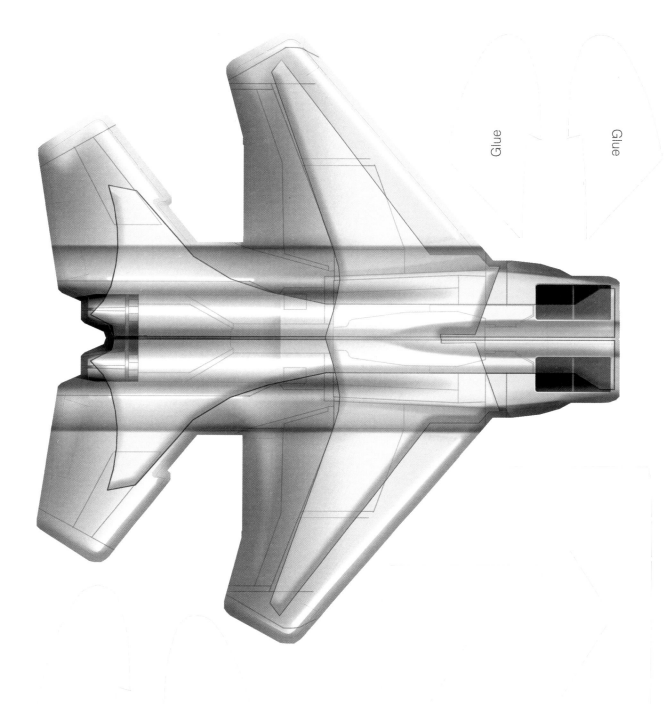

Glue

Glue

Glue

Glue

Glue

Glue

·Remove along the lines and assemble
according to the guide on page 35.

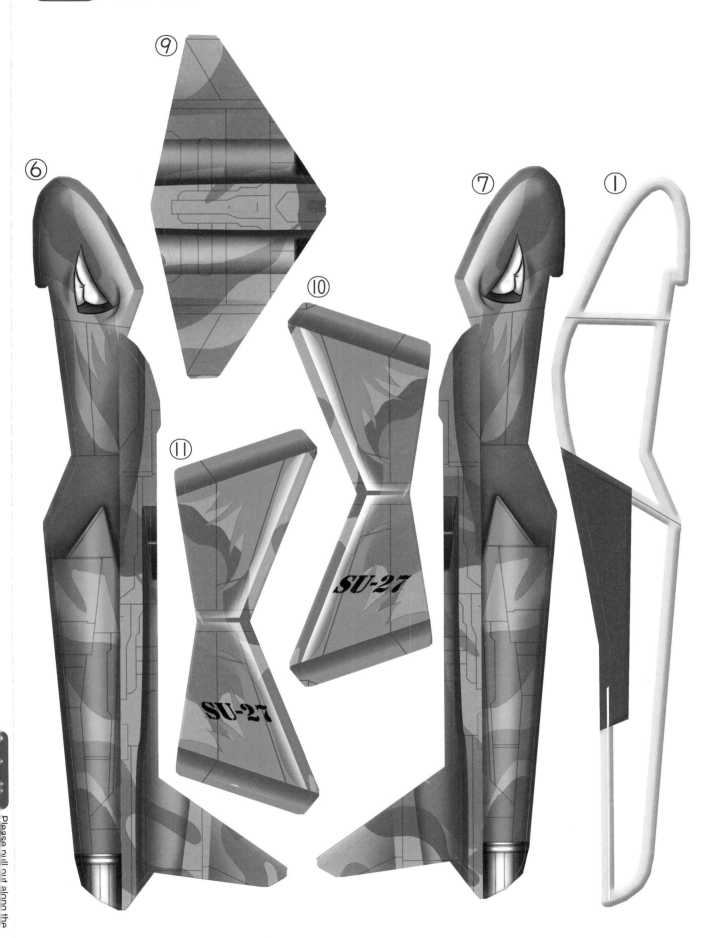

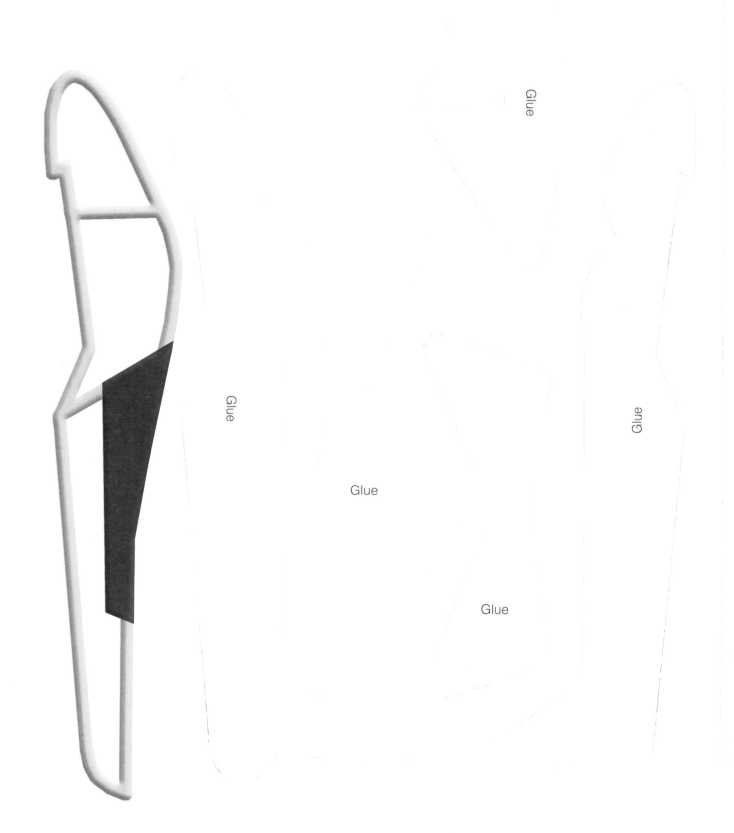

Glue

Glue

Glue

Glue

Glue

**No. 4** SU-27

·Remove along the lines and assemble
according to the guide on page 35.

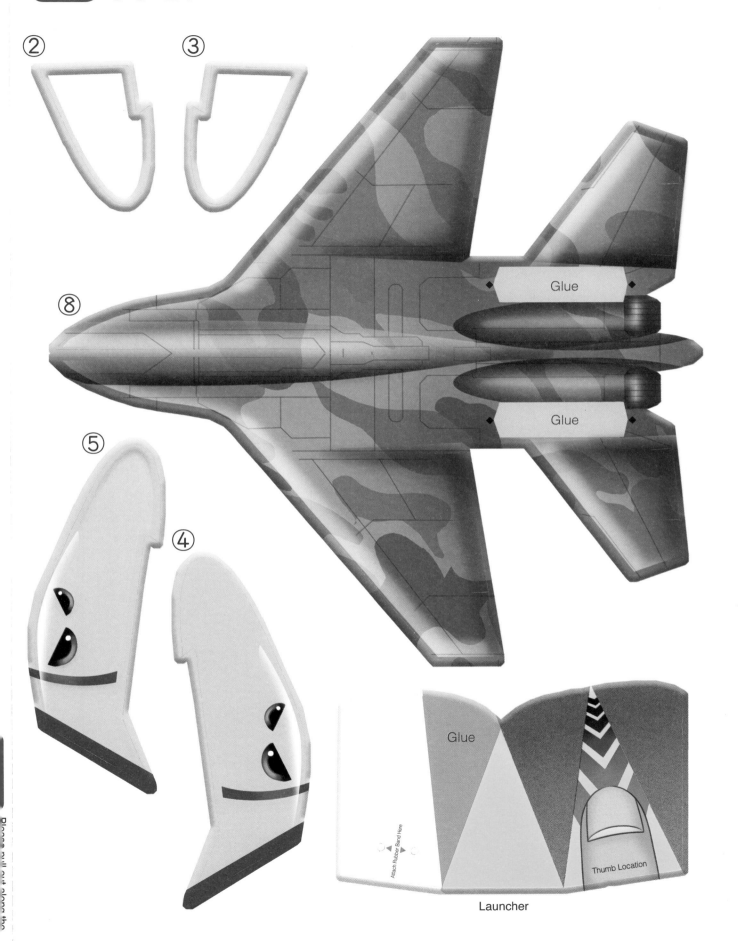

② ③ ⑧ ⑤ ④

Glue

Glue

Glue

Attach Rubber Band Here

Thumb Location

Launcher

Glue

Glue

Glue

Glue

Attach Rubber Band Here

·Remove along the lines and assemble
according to the guide on page 37.

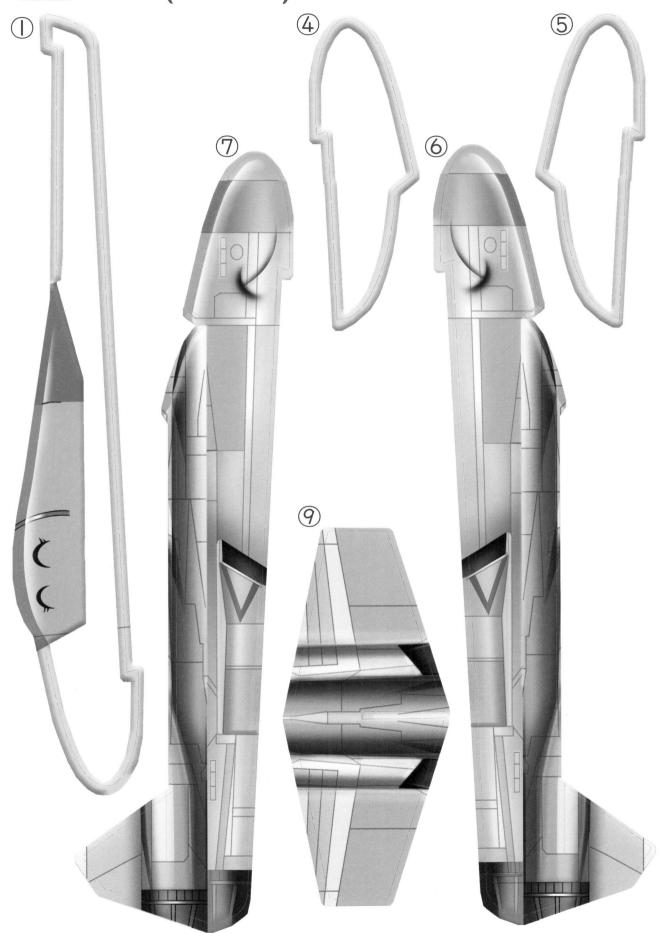

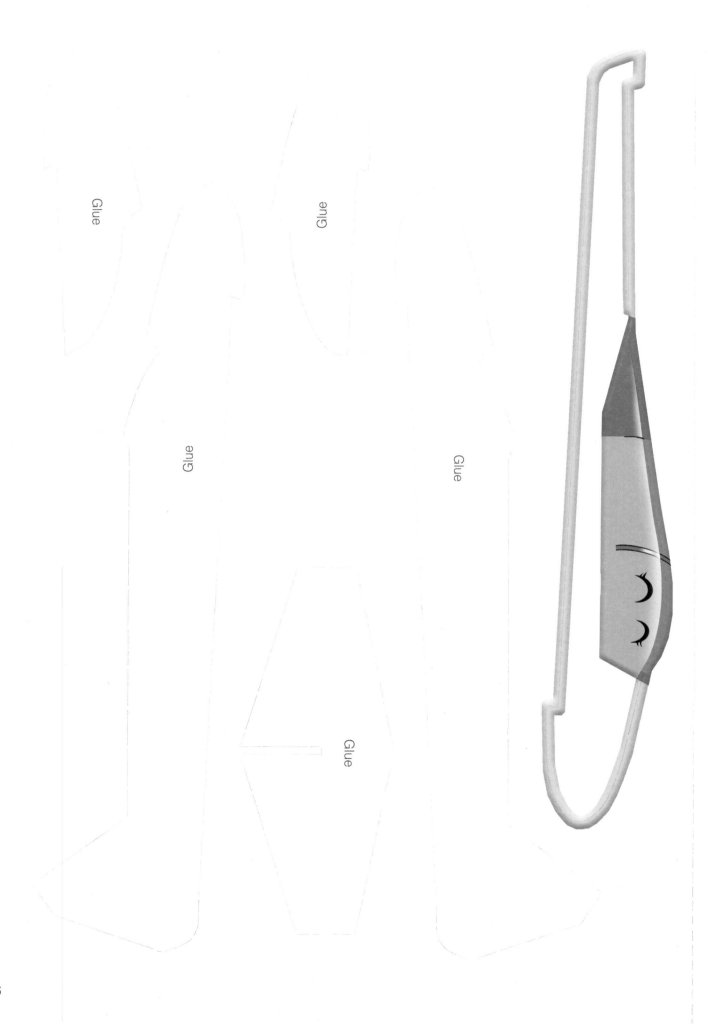

Glue

Glue

Glue

Glue

Glue

66

**F-18 (Hornet)**

·Remove along the lines and assemble
according to the guide on page 37.

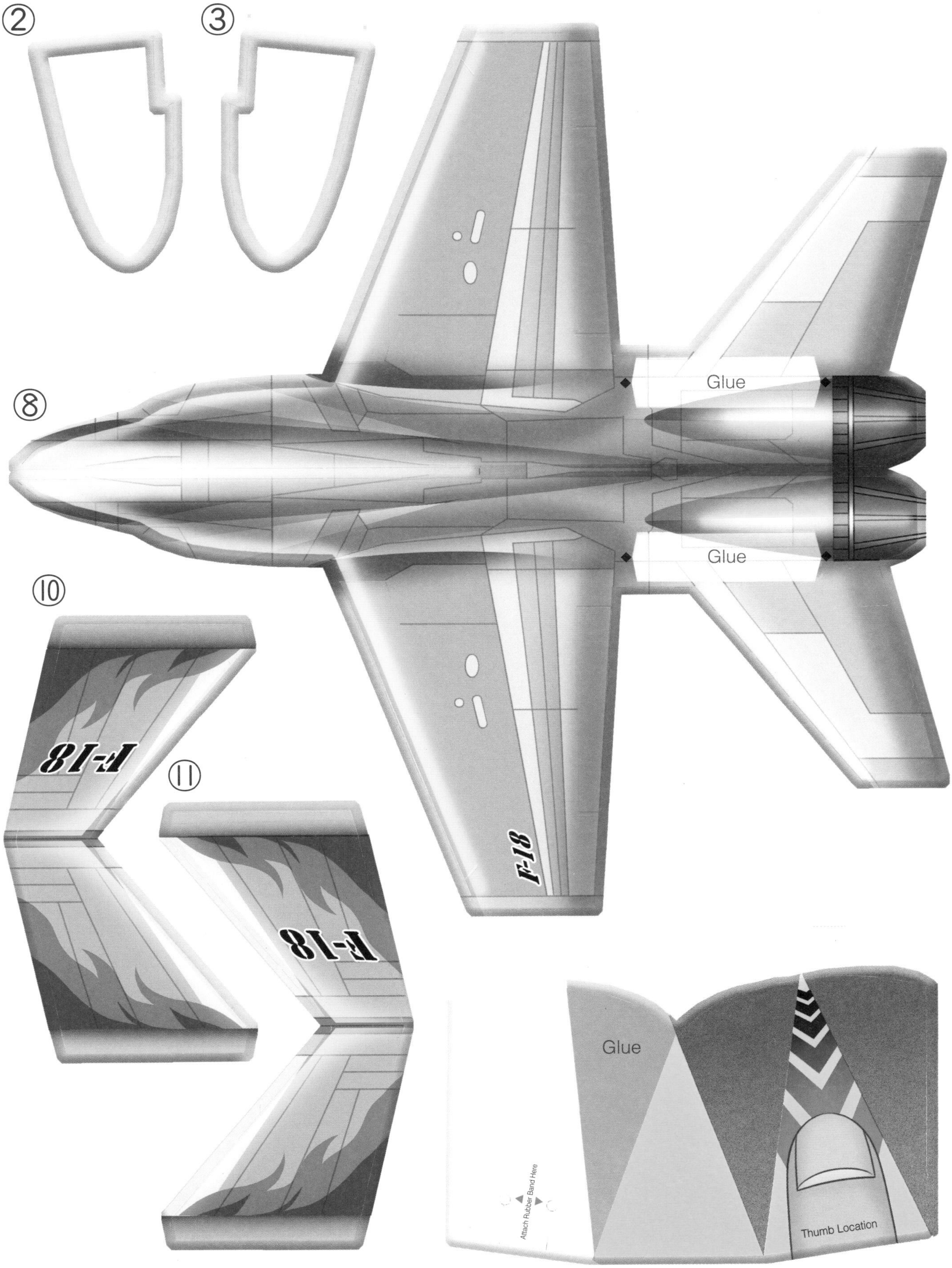

② ③

⑧

⑩

F-18

F-18

⑪

F-18

Glue

Glue

F-18

Glue

Attach Rubber Band Here

Thumb Location

Launcher

Please pull out along the

67

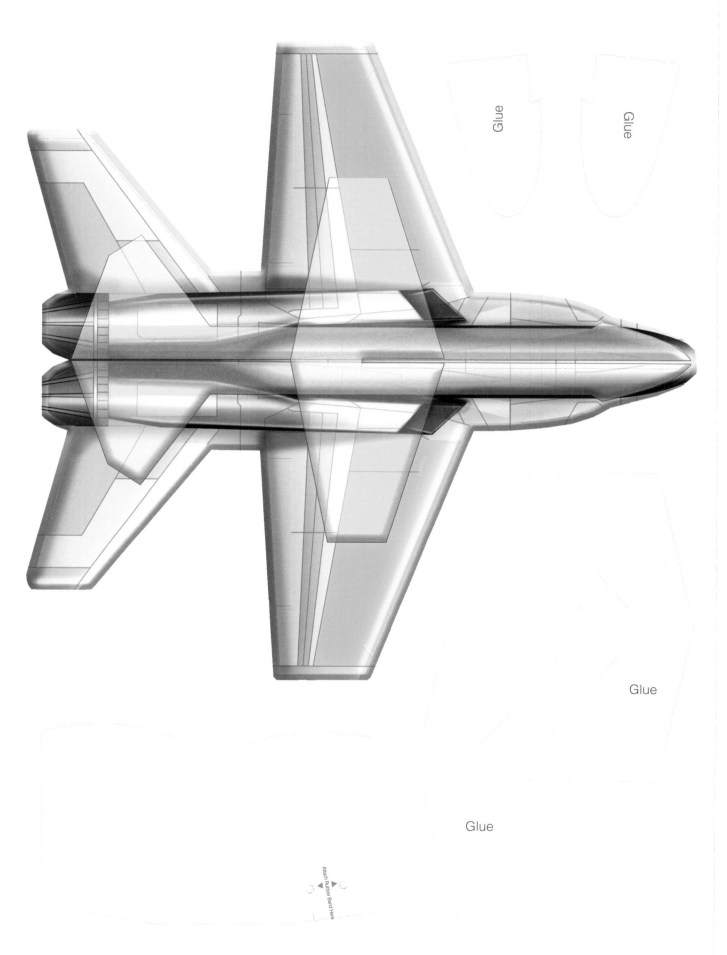

Glue

Glue

Glue

Glue

Attach Rubber Band Here

·Remove along the lines and assemble
according to the guide on page 39.

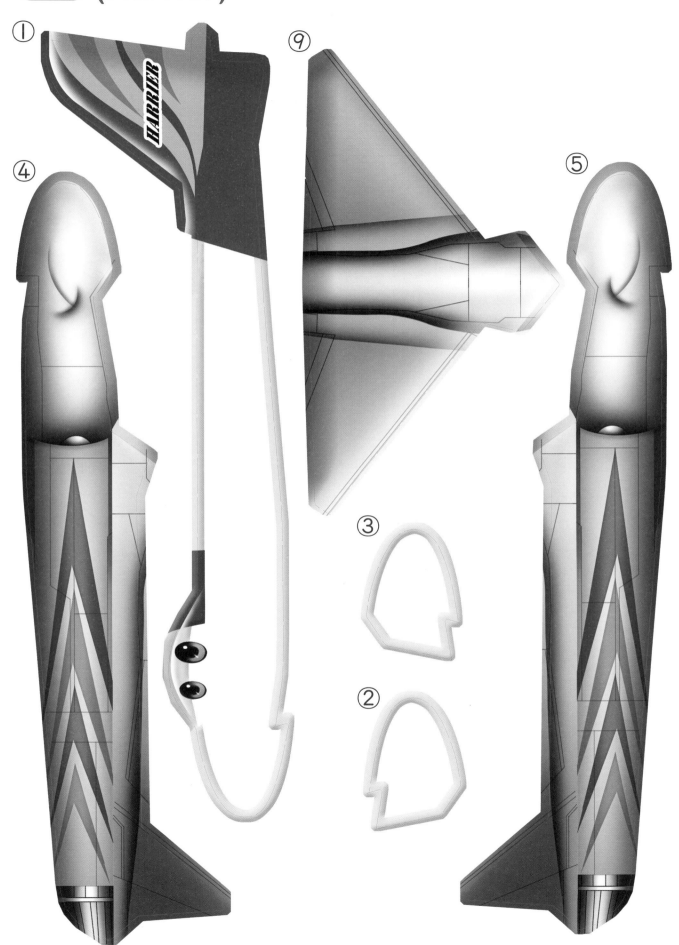

HARRIER

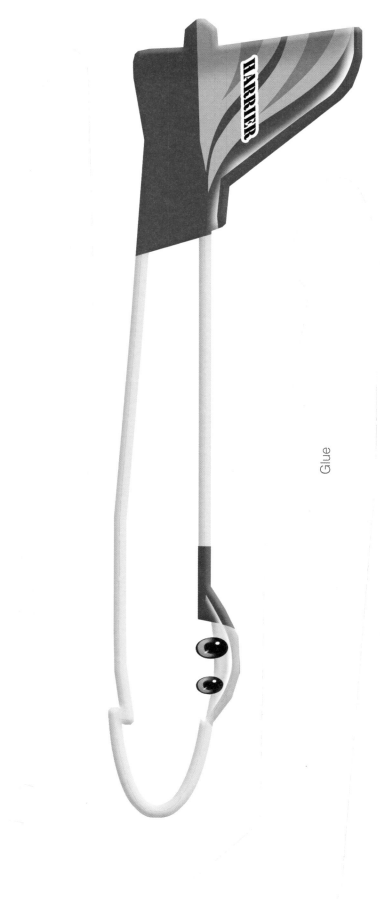

Glue

Glue

Glue

Glue

Glue

Glue

70

## No. 6 (Harrier)

·Remove along the lines and assemble
according to the guide on page 39.

⑧

⑦

⑥

Glue

Attach Rubber Band Here

Thumb Location

Launcher

71

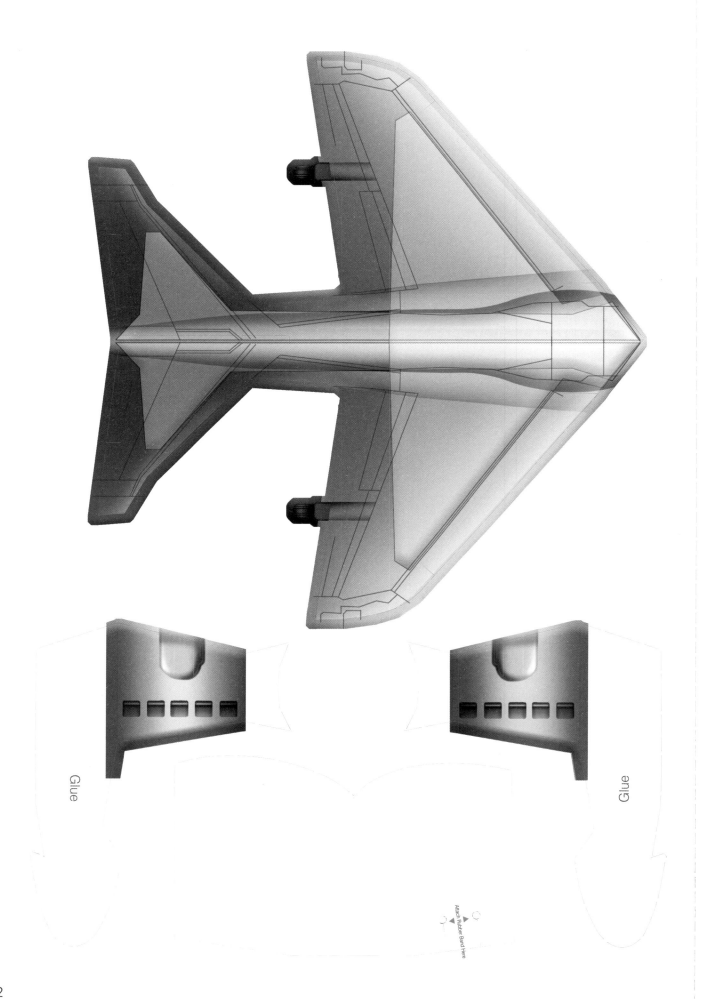

Glue

Glue

Attach Rubber Band Here

·Remove along the lines and assemble
according to the guide on page 41.

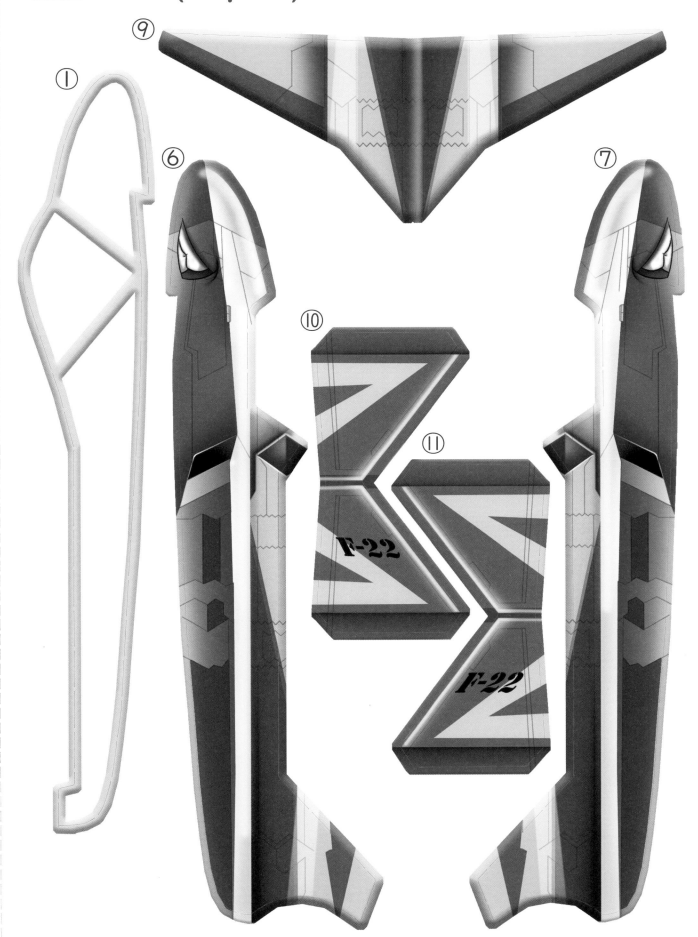

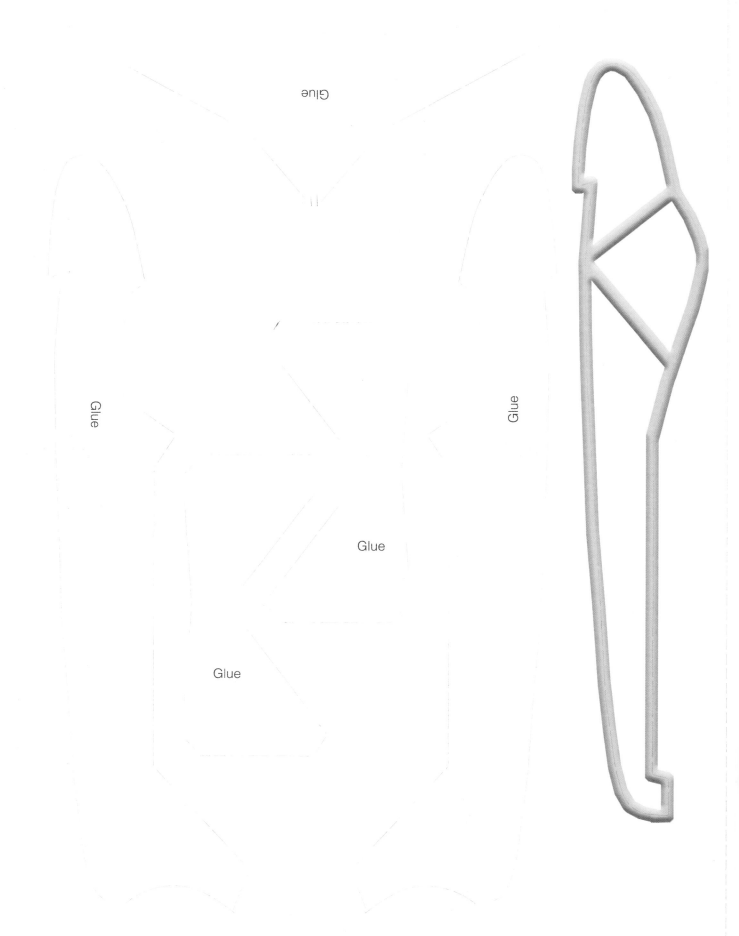

Glue

Glue

Glue

Glue

Glue

# No. 7 F-22 (Raptor)

·Remove along the lines and assemble according to the guide on page 41.

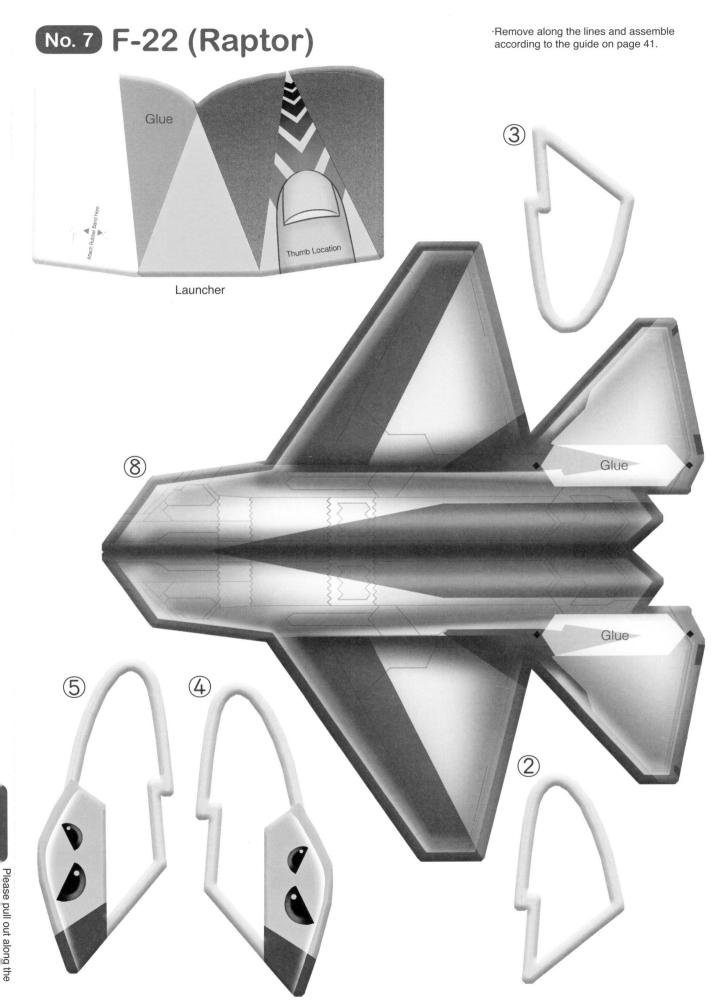

Glue

Attach Rubber Band Here

Thumb Location

Launcher

③

⑧

Glue

Glue

⑤ ④

②

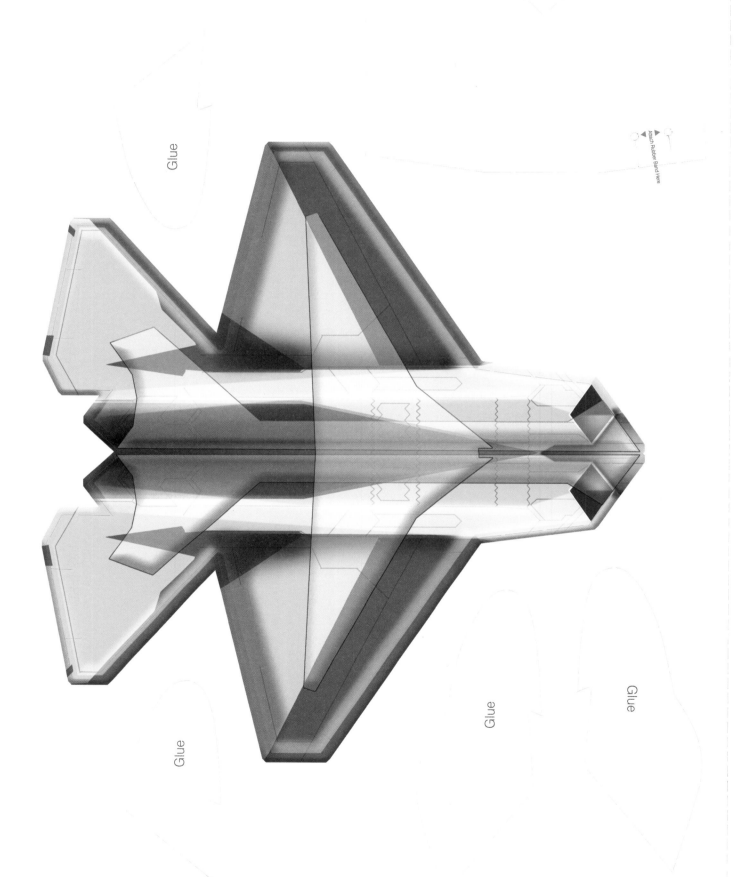

Glue

Glue

Glue

Glue

Attach Rubber Band Here

76

No.8 **Black Eagle**

·Remove along the lines and assemble according to the guide on page 43.

77

Glue

Glue

Glue

BLACK EAGLE

·Remove along the lines and assemble according to the guide on page 43.

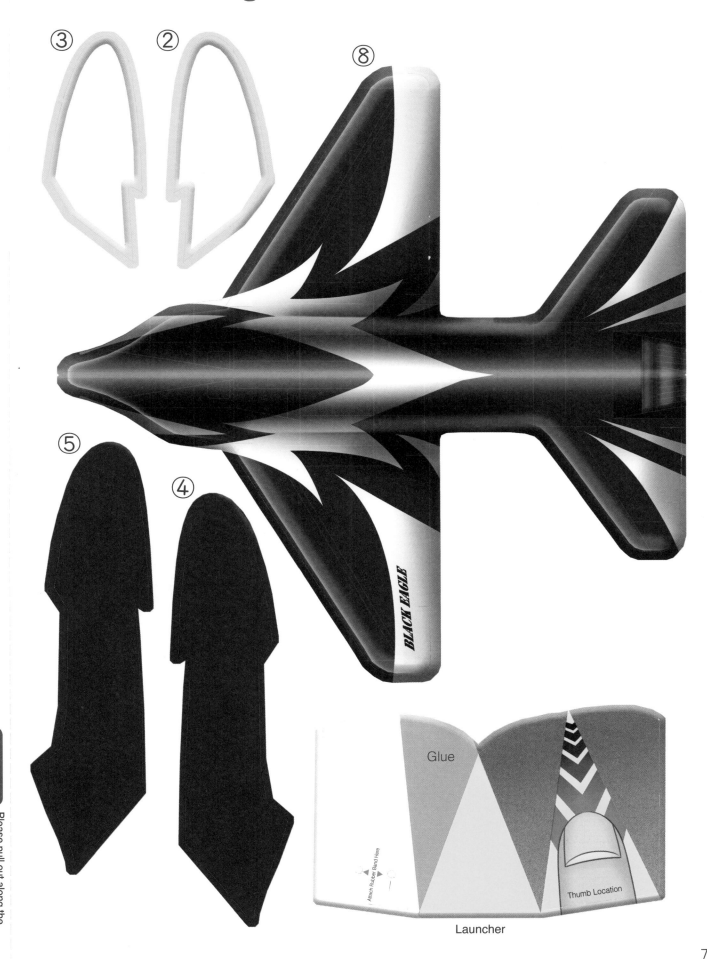

③ ② ⑧

⑤ ④

BLACK EAGLE

Glue

Attach Rubber Band Here

Thumb Location

Launcher

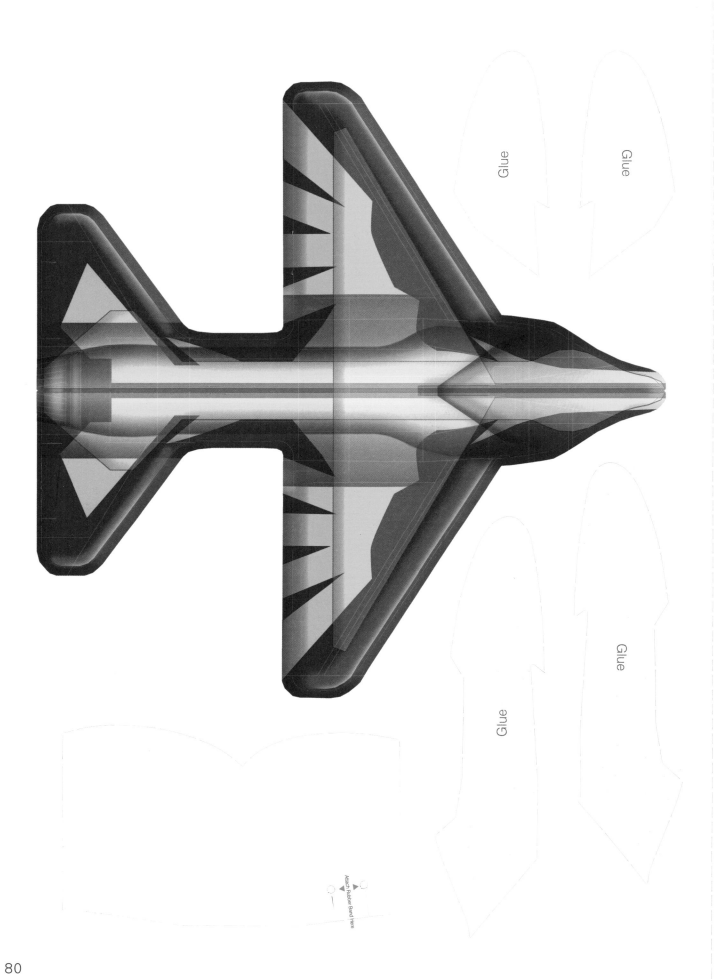

Glue

Glue

Glue

Glue

Attach Rubber Band Here

VTOL Drone "Joy"

·Remove along the lines and assemble according to the guide on page 45.

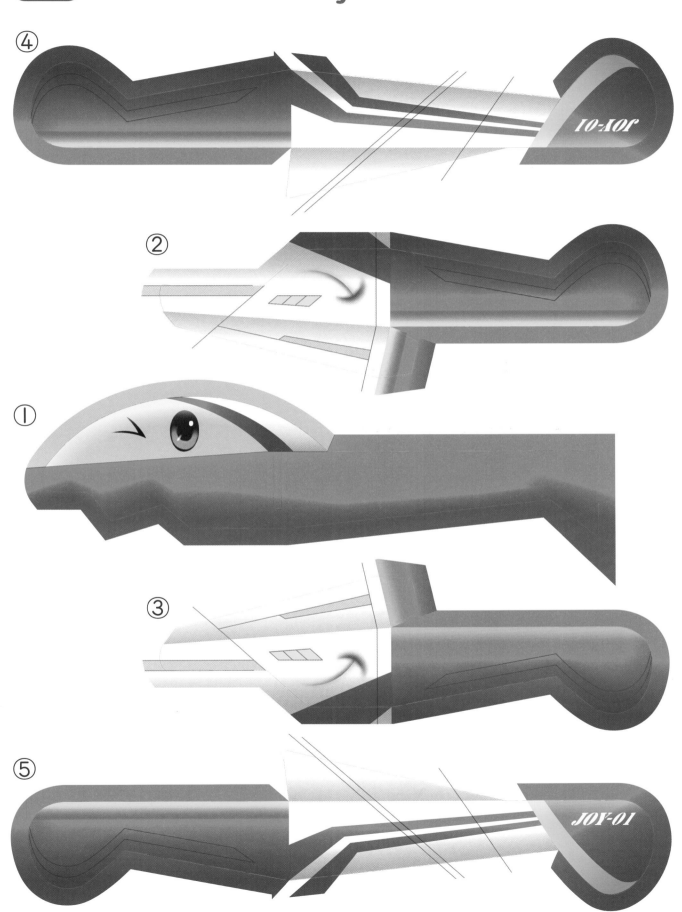

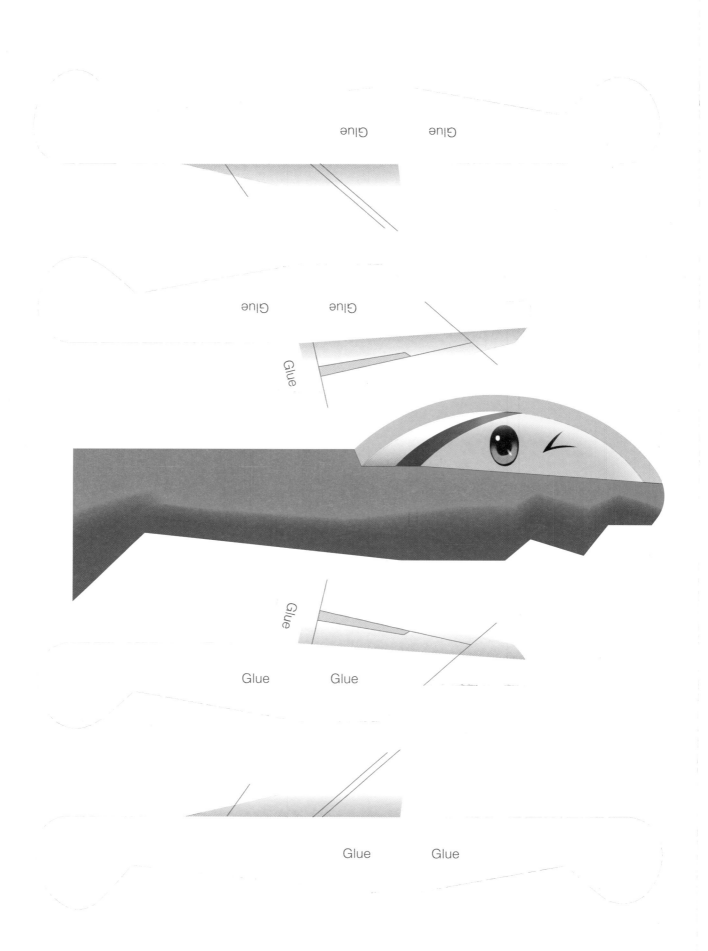

Glue    Glue

Glue    Glue

Glue

Glue

Glue    Glue

Glue    Glue

82

**VTOL Drone "Joy"**

·Remove along the lines and assemble according to the guide on page 45.

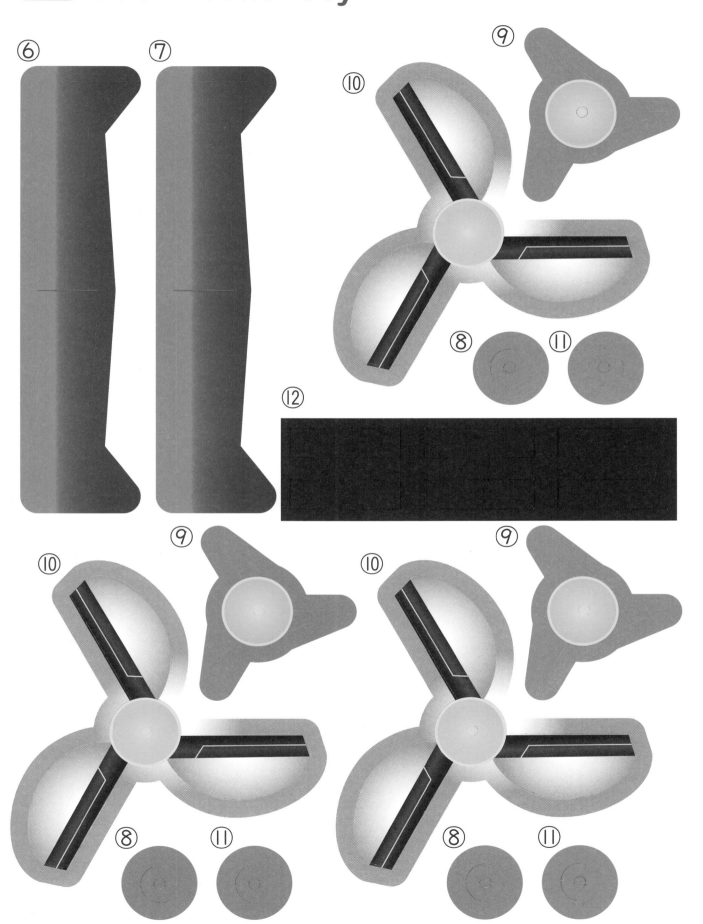

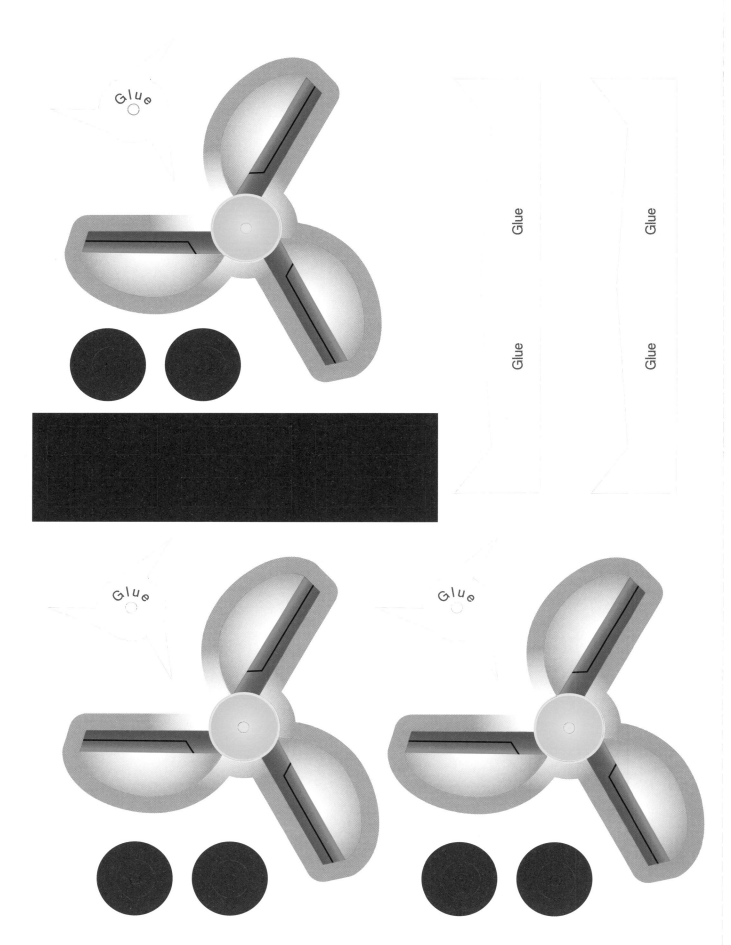

# No. 1 Super Glider

·Remove along the lines and assemble according to the guide on page 29.

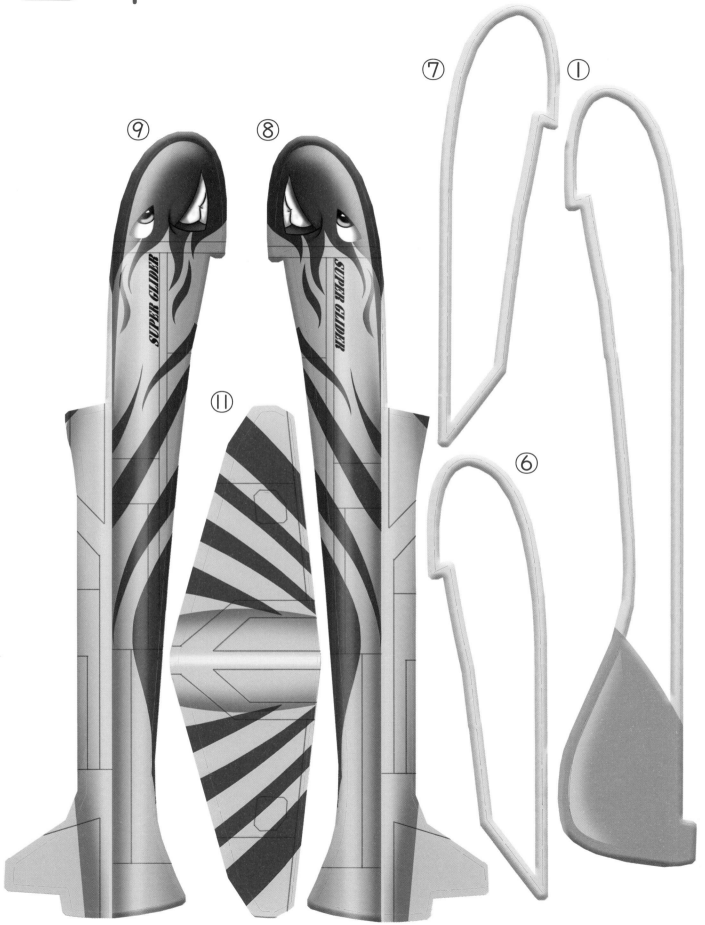

85

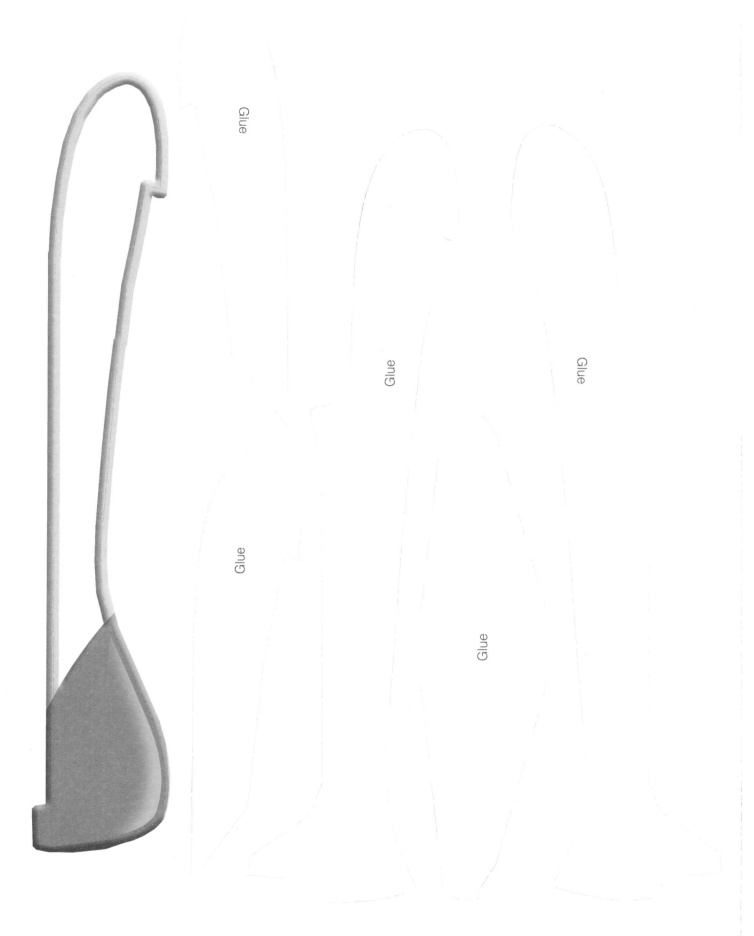

Glue

Glue

Glue

Glue

Glue

Glue

# No. 1 Super Glider

·Remove along the lines and assemble according to the guide on page 29.

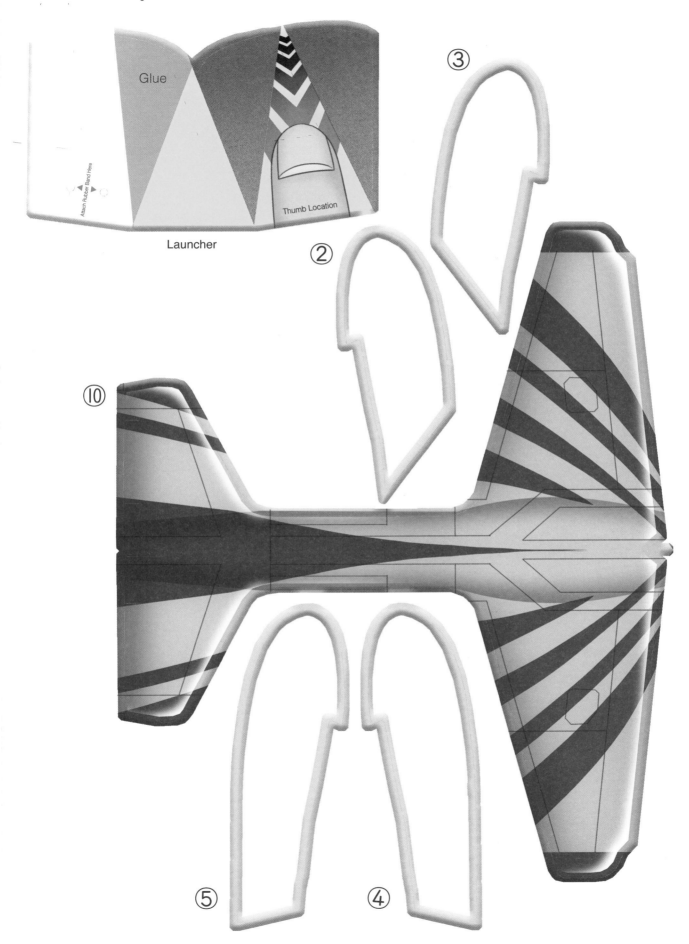

Glue

Attach Rubber Band Here

Thumb Location

Launcher

③

②

⑩

⑤

④

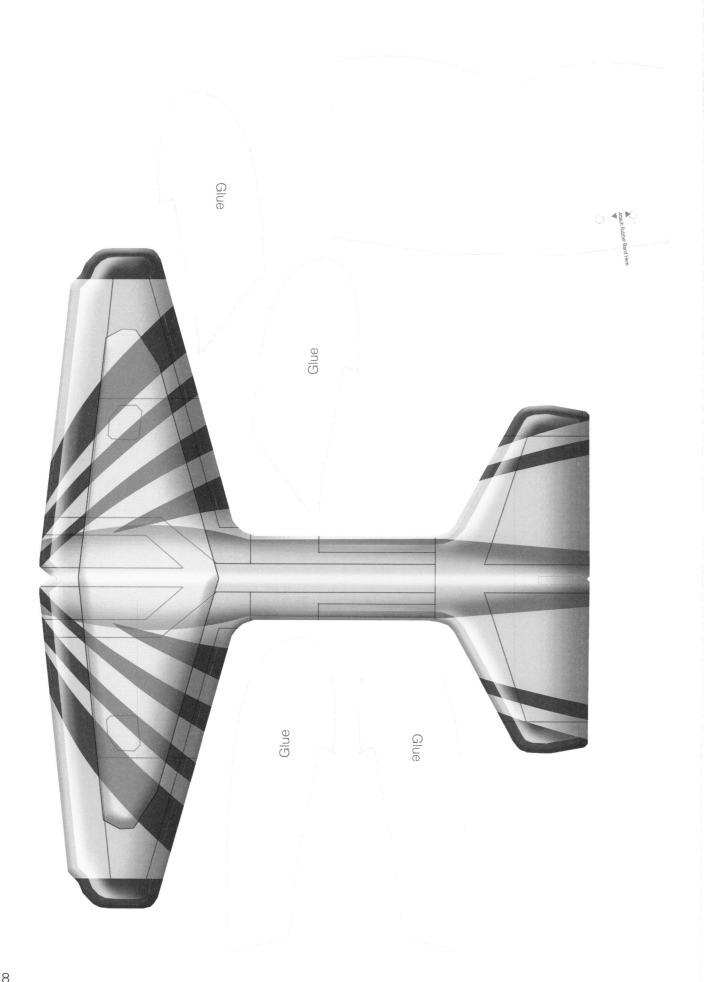

Glue

Glue

Glue

Glue

Attach Rubber Band Here

T-50 (Golden Eagle)

·Remove along the lines and assemble
according to the guide on page 31.

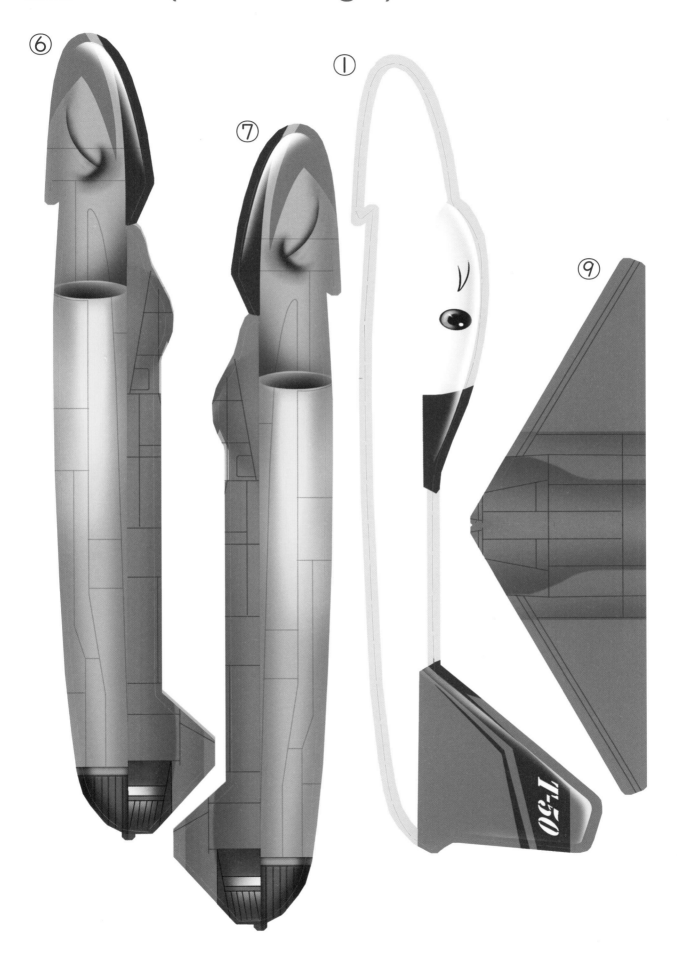

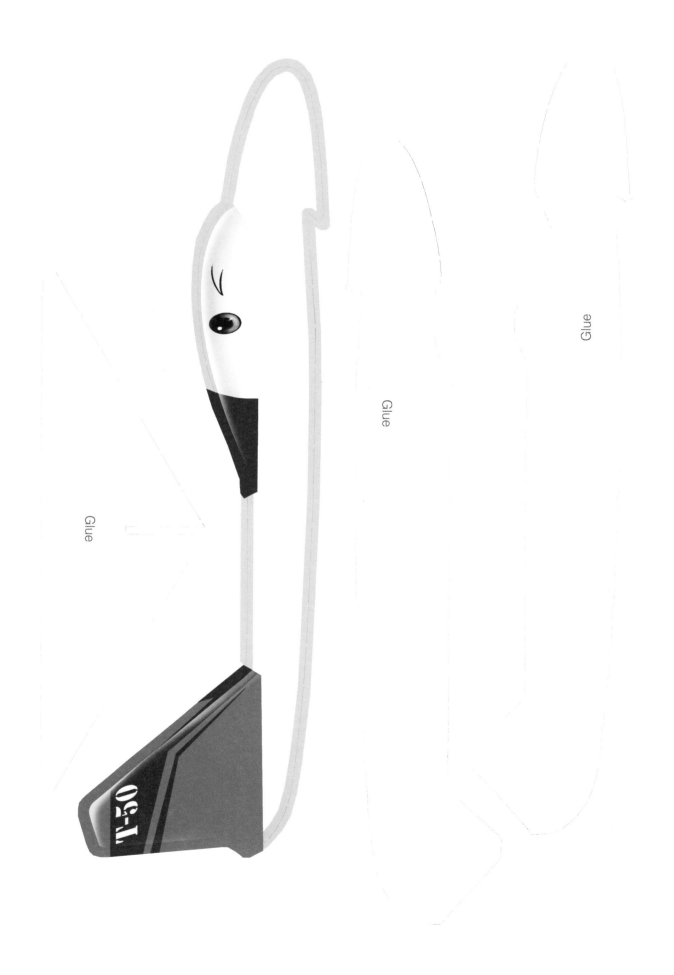

Glue

Glue

Glue

T-50

# T-50 (Golden Eagle)

·Remove along the lines and assemble
according to the guide on page 31.

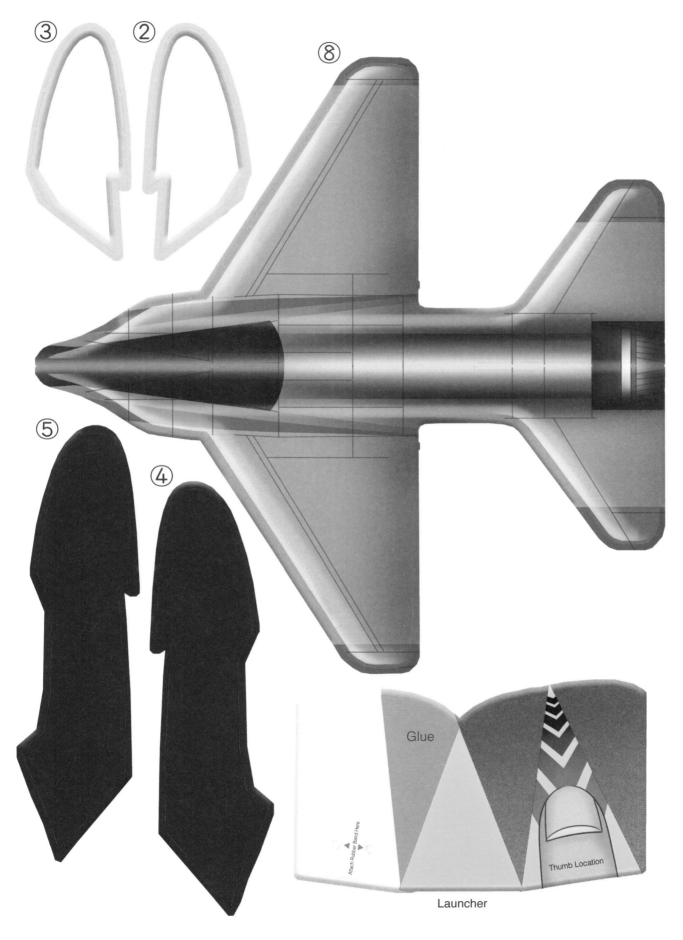

③ ② ⑧

⑤ ④

Glue

Attach Rubber Band Here

Thumb Location

Launcher

Please pull out along the

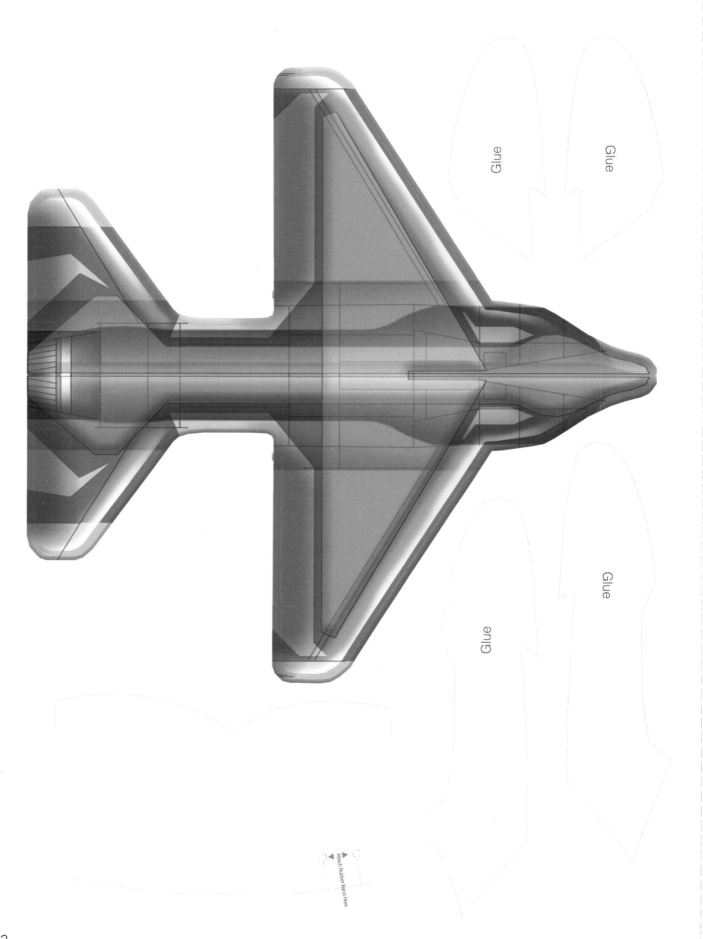

Glue

Glue

Glue

Glue

Attach Rubber Band Here

# No. 3 F-15 (Eagle)

·Remove along the lines and assemble according to the guide on page 33.

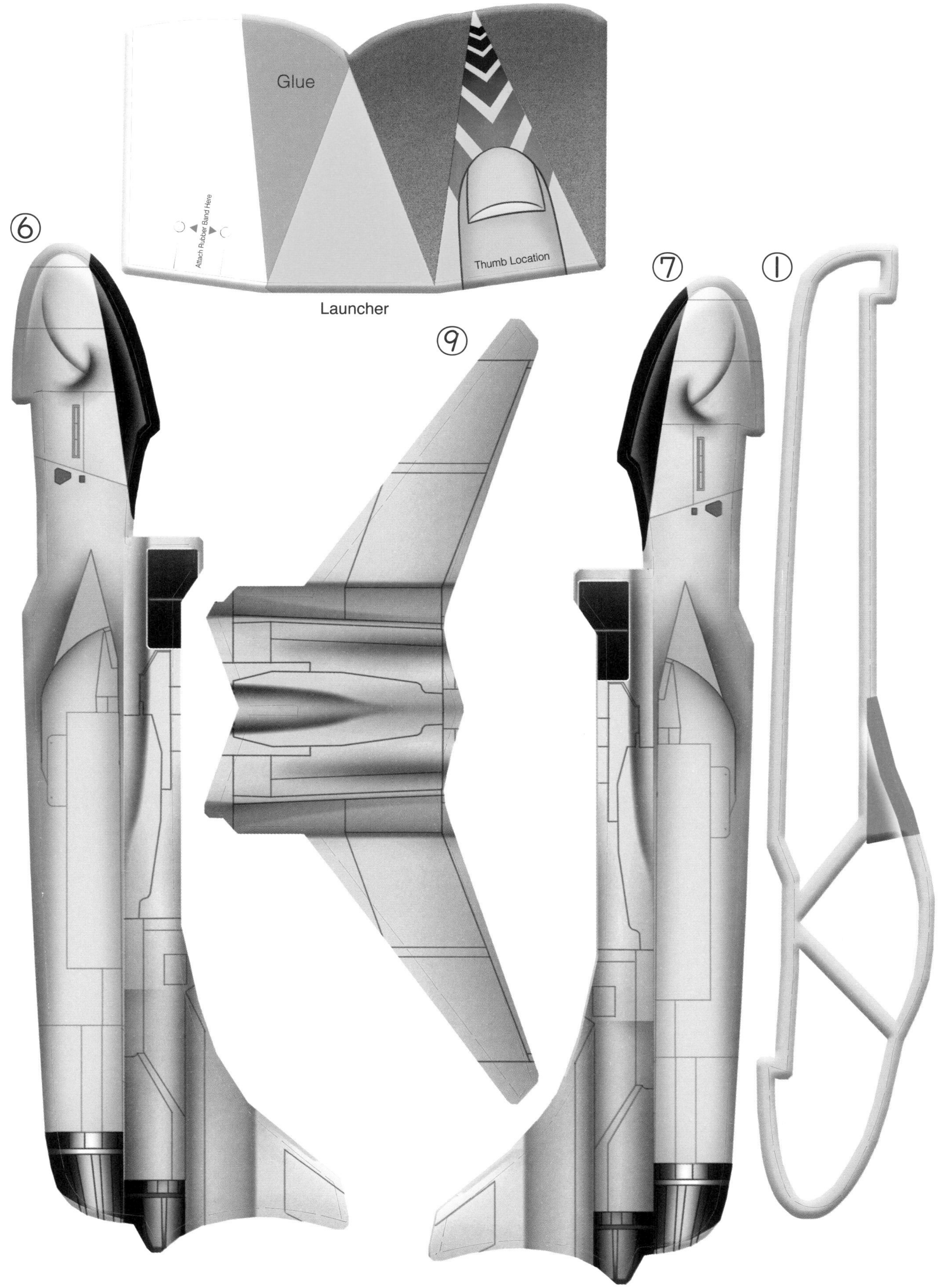

Glue
Attach Rubber Band Here
Thumb Location
Launcher
⑥
⑨
⑦
①


Please pull out along the

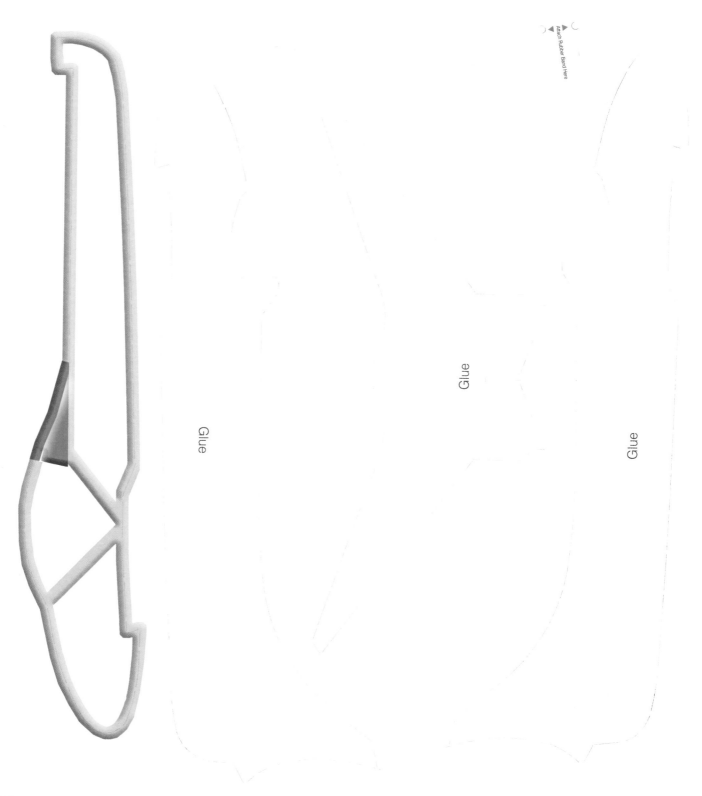

Glue

Glue

Glue

Attach Rubber Band Here

·Remove along the lines and assemble
according to the guide on page 33.

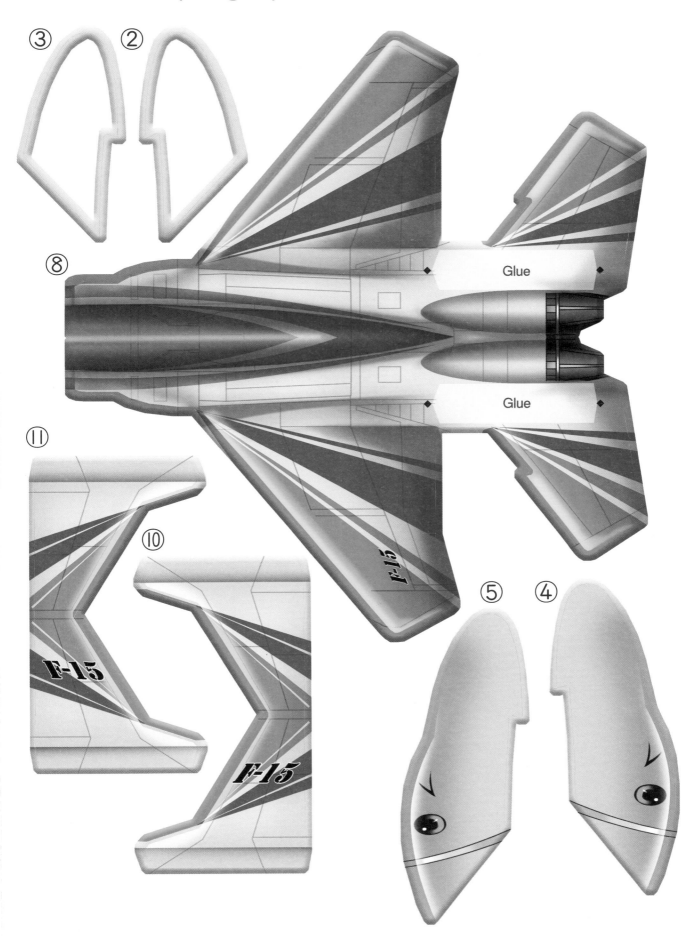

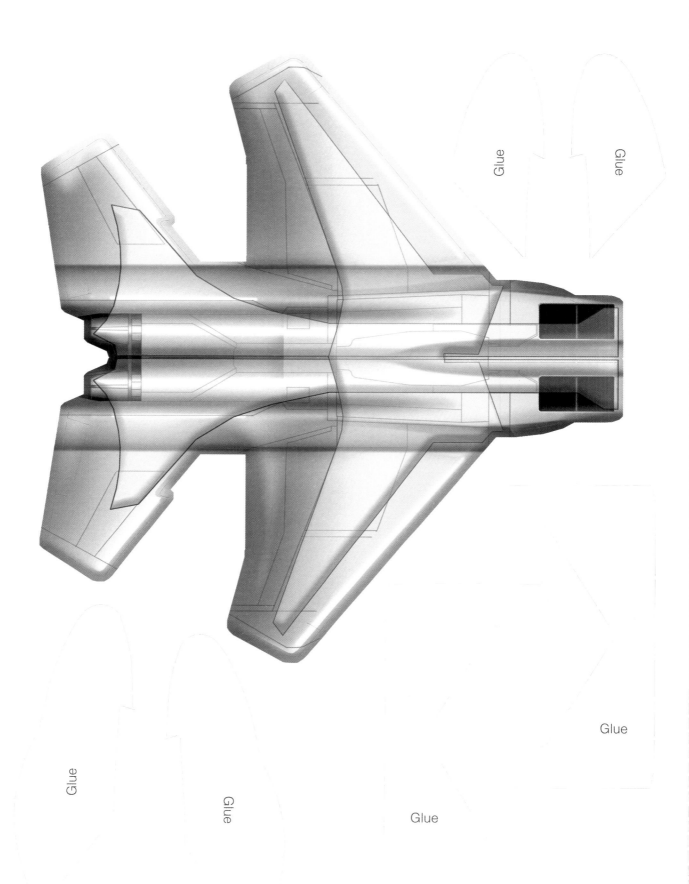

Glue

Glue

Glue

Glue

Glue

Glue

·Remove along the lines and assemble according to the guide on page 35.

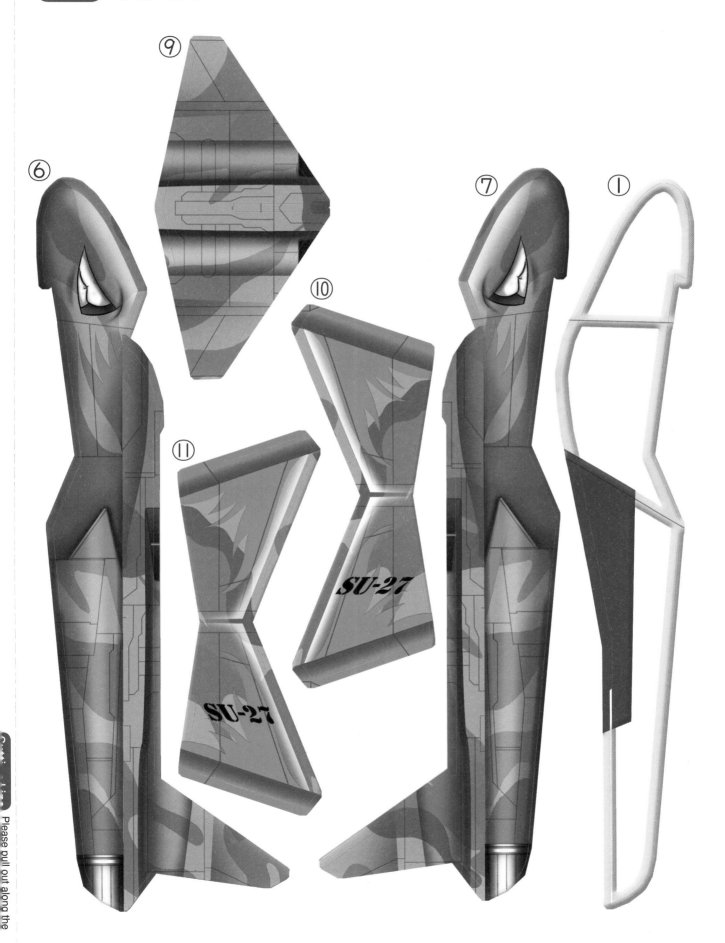

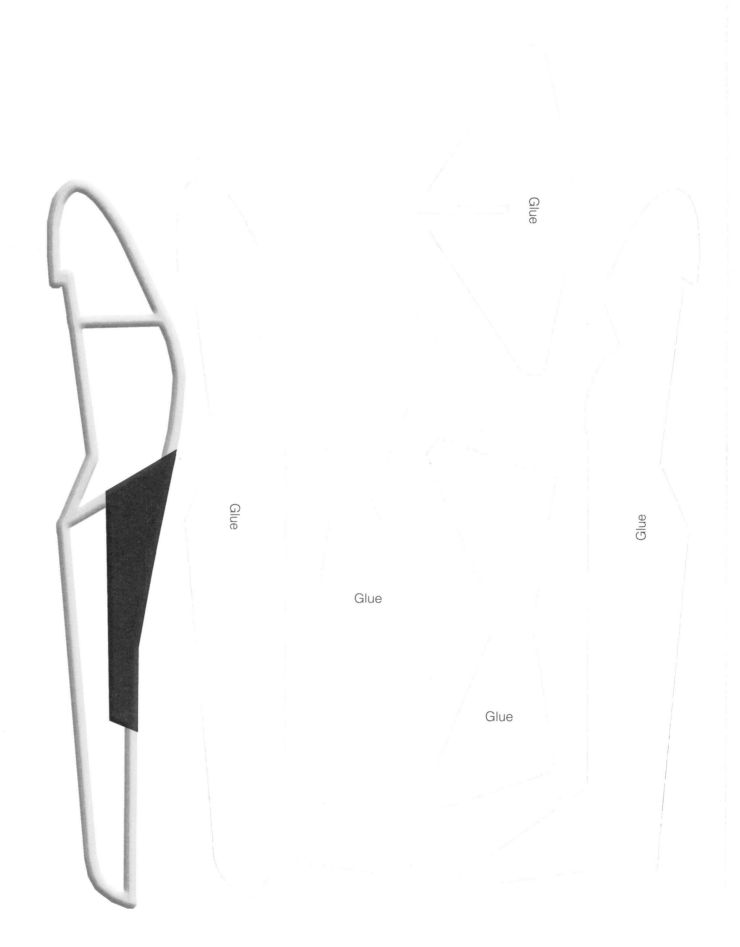

Glue

Glue

Glue

Glue

Glue

·Remove along the lines and assemble according to the guide on page 35.

② ③

⑧

⑤

④

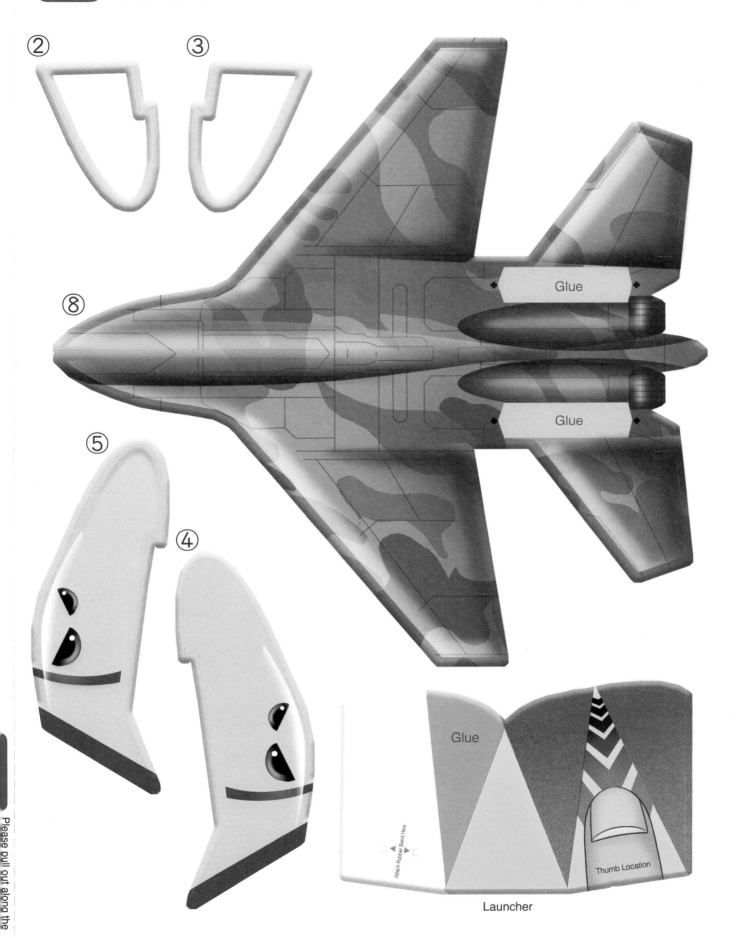

Glue

Glue

Glue

Attach Rubber Band Here

Thumb Location

Launcher

Please pull out along the

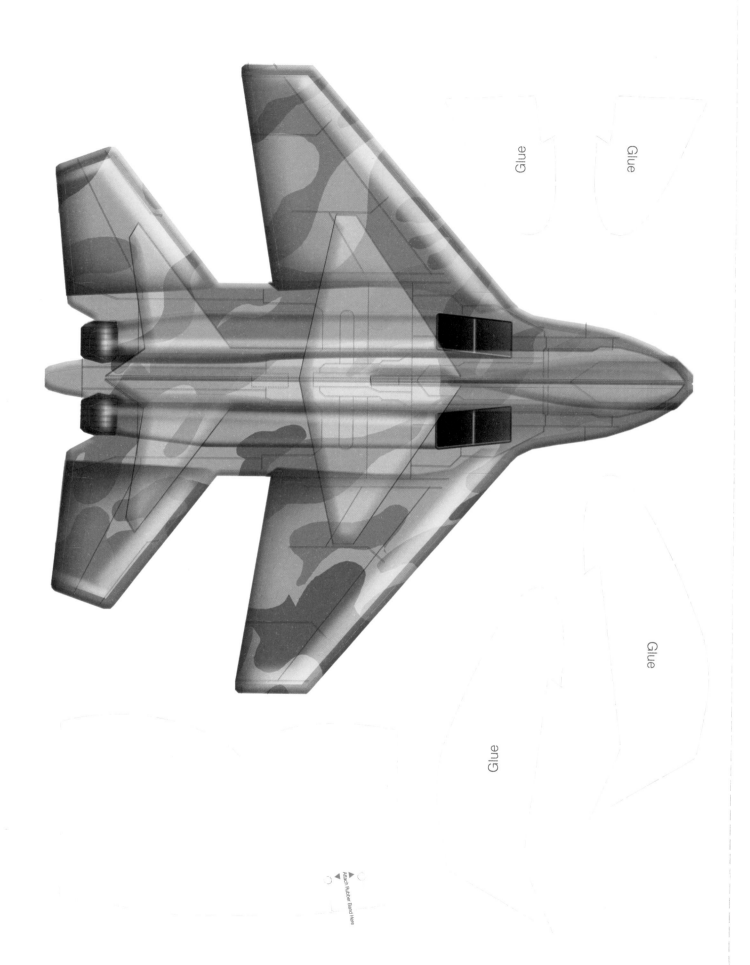

Glue

Glue

Glue

Glue

Attach Rubber Band Here

**F-18 (Hornet)**

·Remove along the lines and assemble according to the guide on page 37.

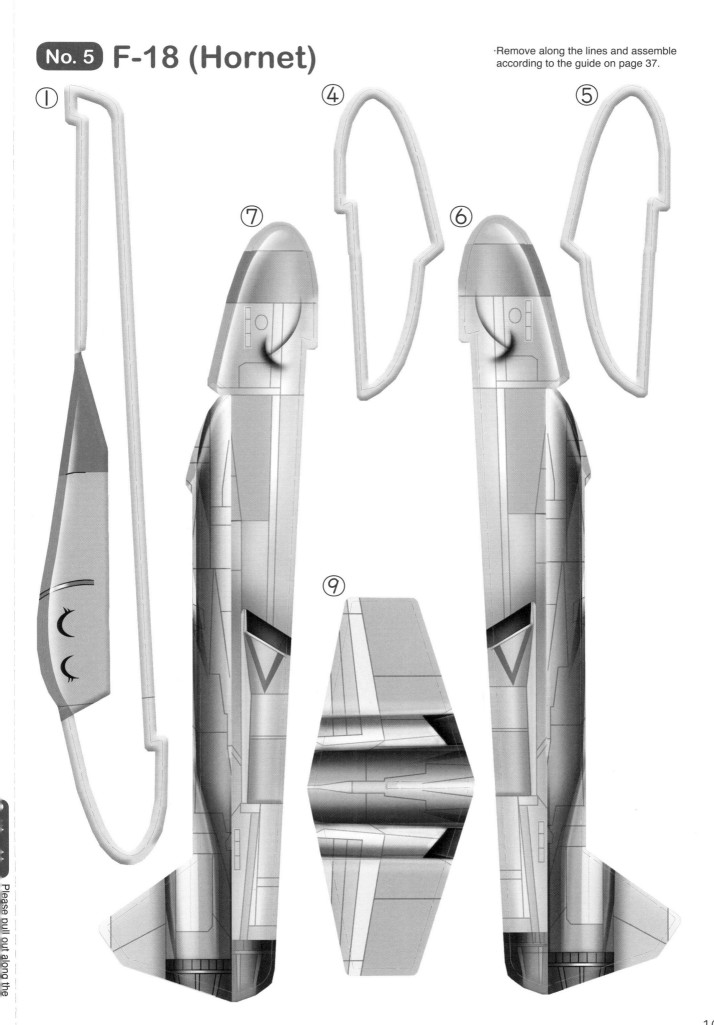

Please pull out along the

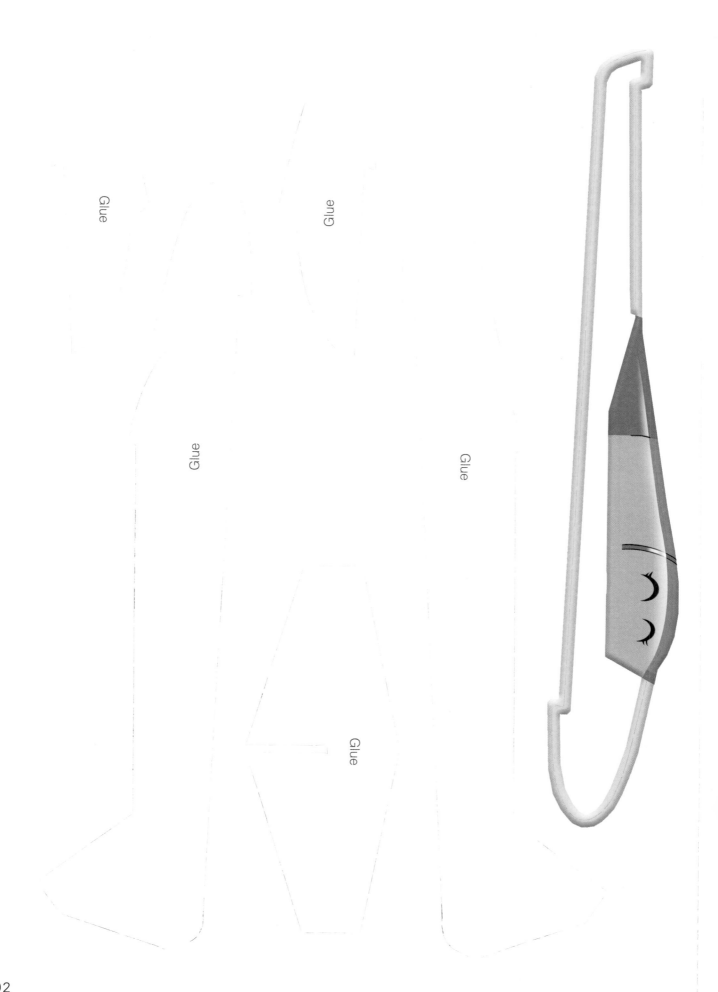

Glue

Glue

Glue

Glue

Glue

# F-18 (Hornet)

·Remove along the lines and assemble according to the guide on page 37.

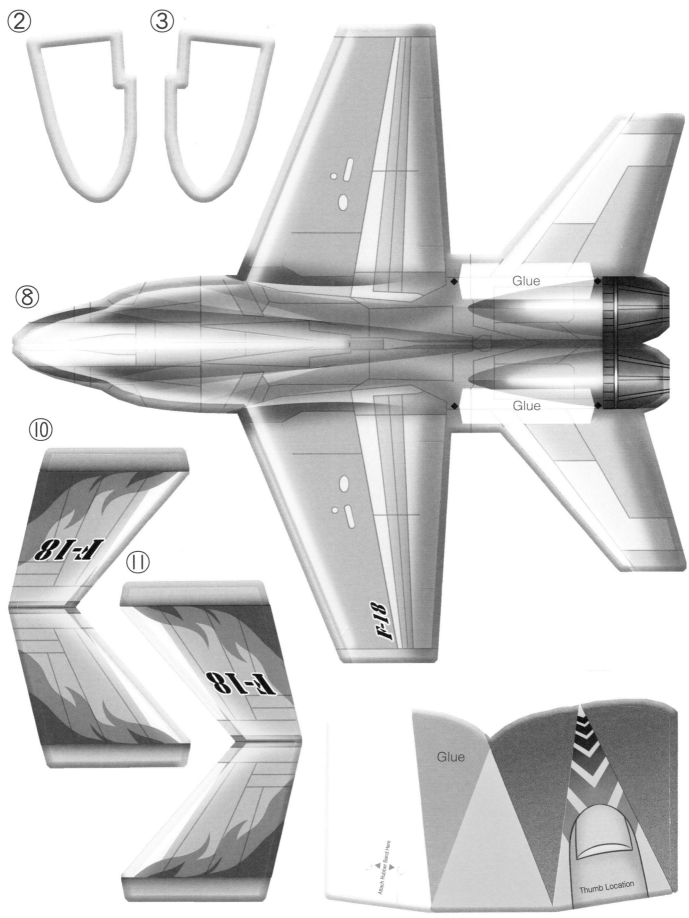

② ③ ⑧ ⑩ ⑪

Glue

Glue

Glue

Attach Rubber Band Here

Thumb Location

Launcher

F-18

Cutting Line Please pull out along the

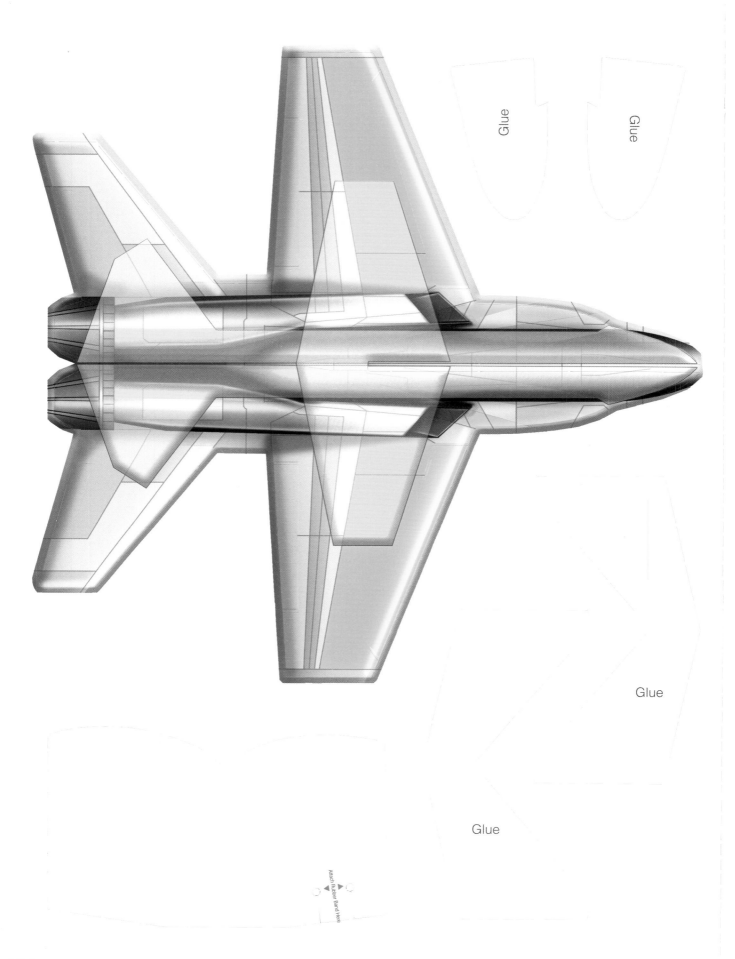

Glue

Glue

Glue

Glue

Attach Rubber Band Here

# No. 6 (Harrier)

·Remove along the lines and assemble according to the guide on page 39.

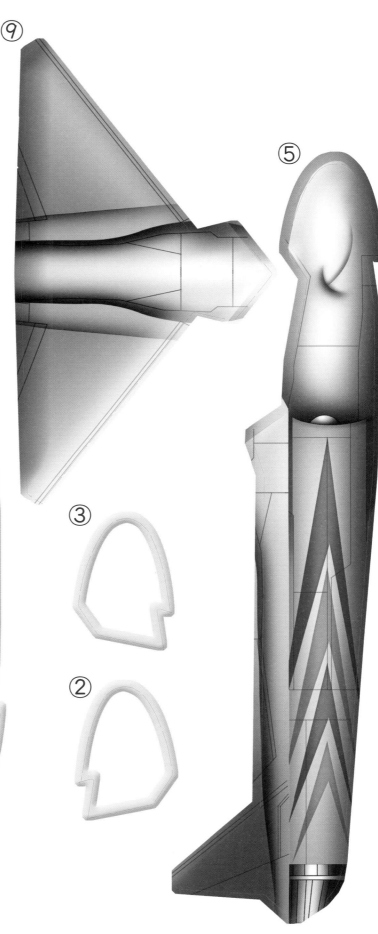

HARRIER

① ④ ⑨ ⑤ ③ ②

Glue

Glue

Glue

Glue

Glue

Glue

·Remove along the lines and assemble according to the guide on page 39.

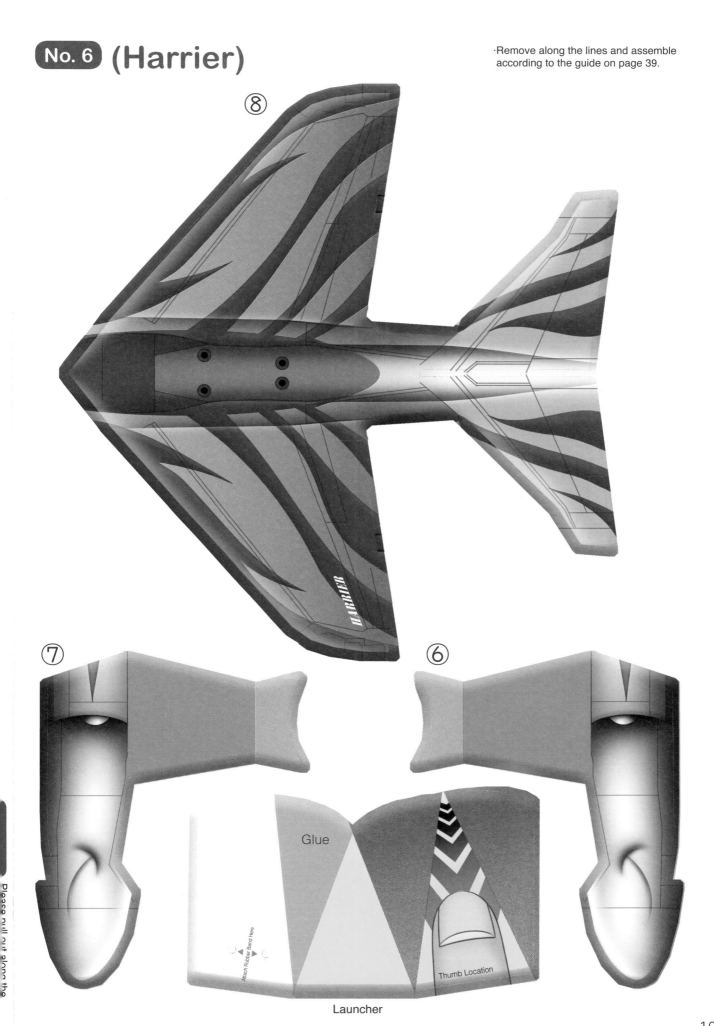

⑧

⑦

⑥

Glue

Attach Rubber Band Here

Thumb Location

Launcher

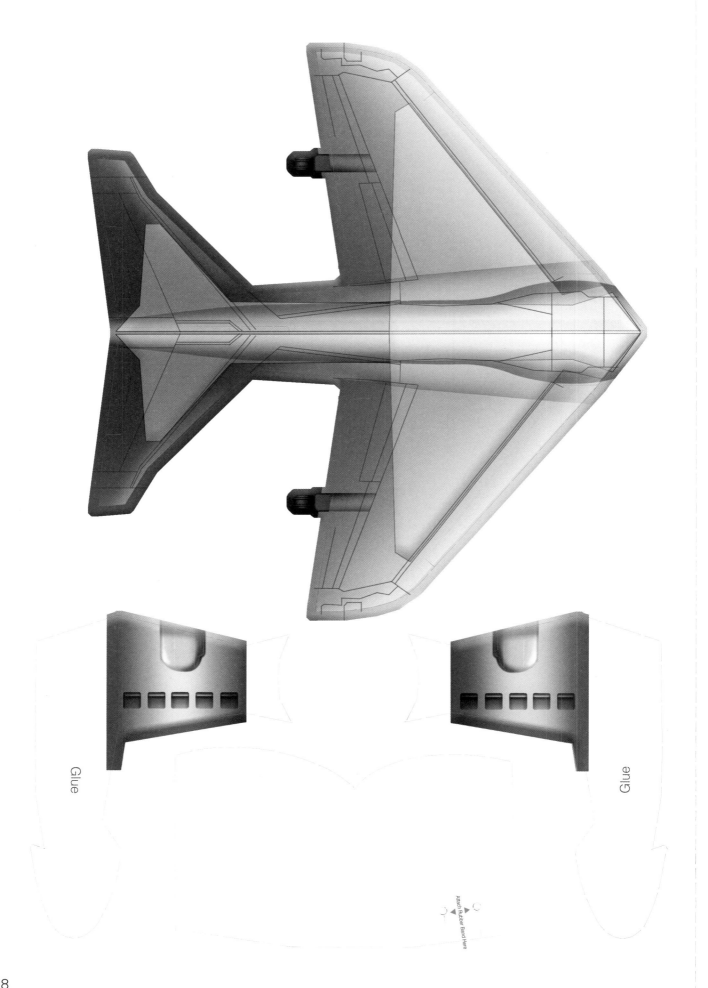

Glue

Glue

Attach Rubber Band Here

·Remove along the lines and assemble
according to the guide on page 41.

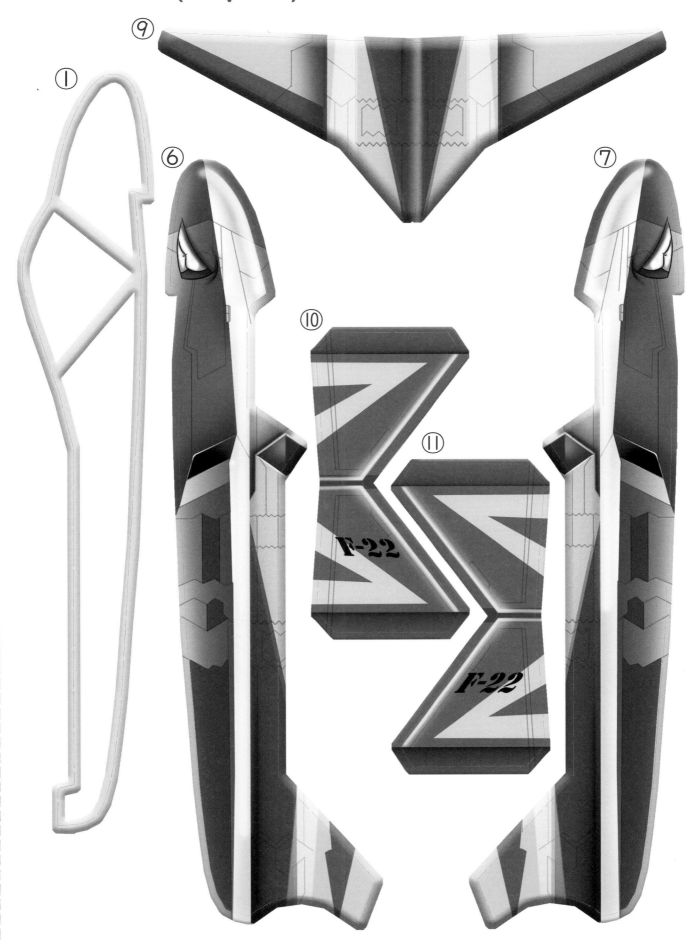

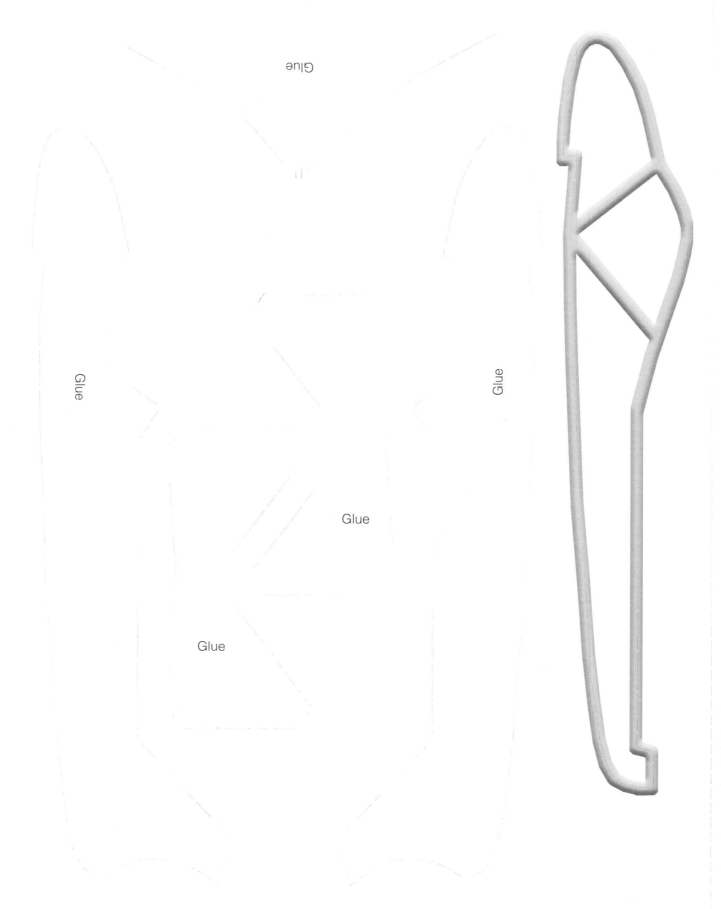

Glue

Glue

Glue

Glue

Glue

·Remove along the lines and assemble according to the guide on page 41.

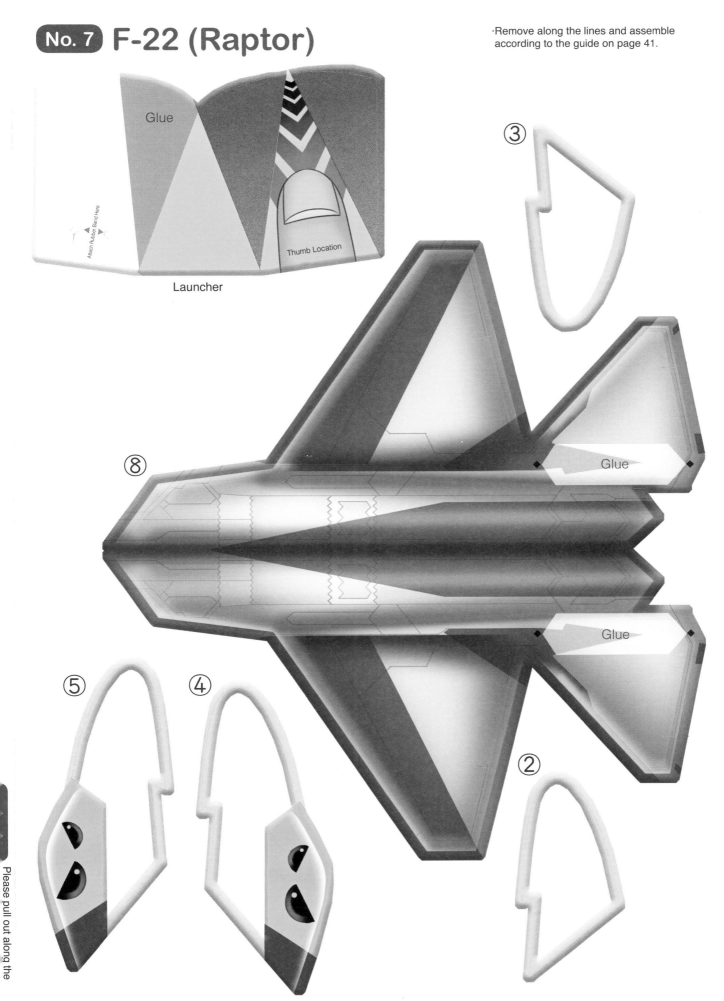

Glue

Attach Rubber Band Here

Thumb Location

Launcher

③

Glue

⑧

Glue

⑤ ④

②

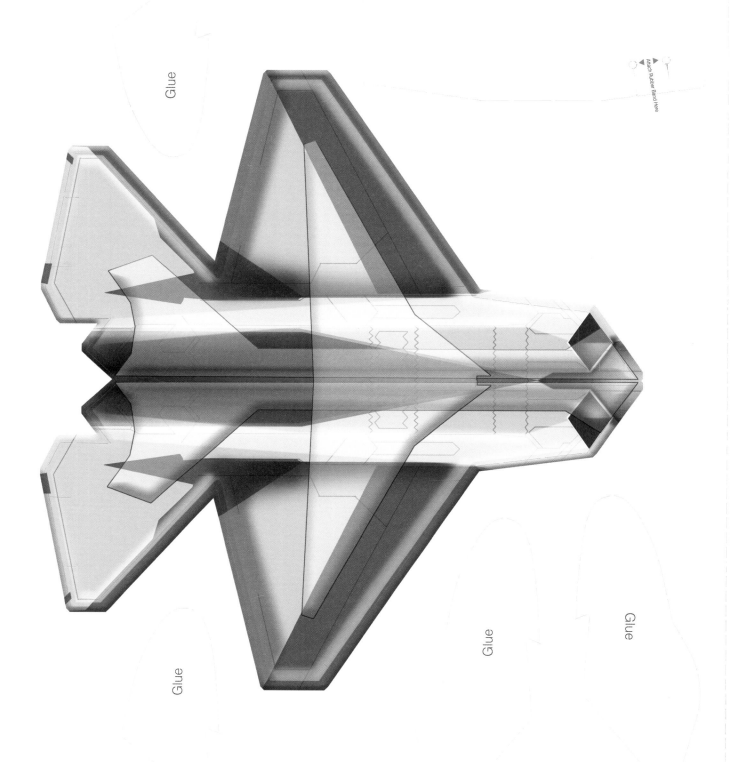

Glue

Glue

Glue

Glue

Attach Rubber Band Here

·Remove along the lines and assemble according to the guide on page 43.

BLACK EAGLE

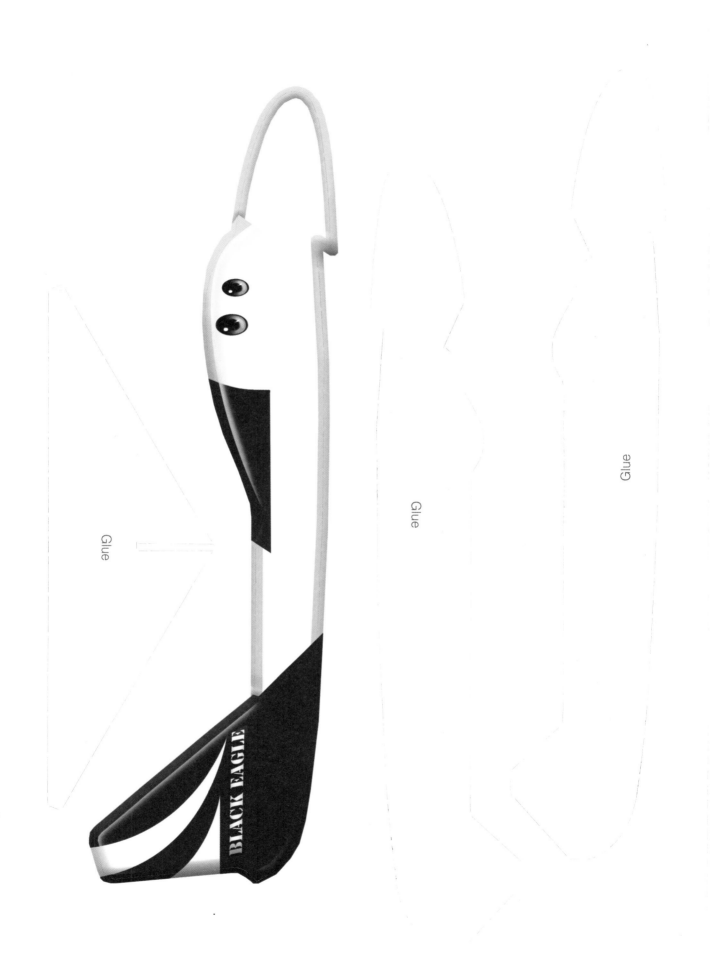

Glue

Glue

Glue

BLACK EAGLE

·Remove along the lines and assemble according to the guide on page 43.

③

②

⑧

⑤

④

Glue

Attach Rubber Band Here

Thumb Location

Launcher

Please pull out along the

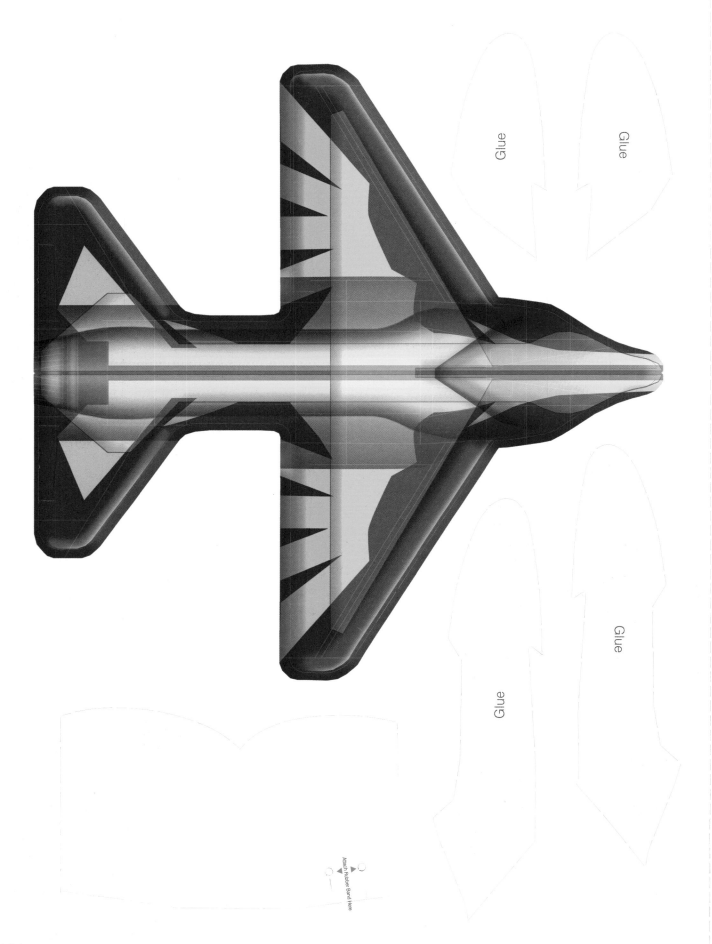

Glue

Glue

Glue

Glue

Attach Rubber Band Here

# No. 9 VTOL Drone "Joy"

·Remove along the lines and assemble according to the guide on page 45.

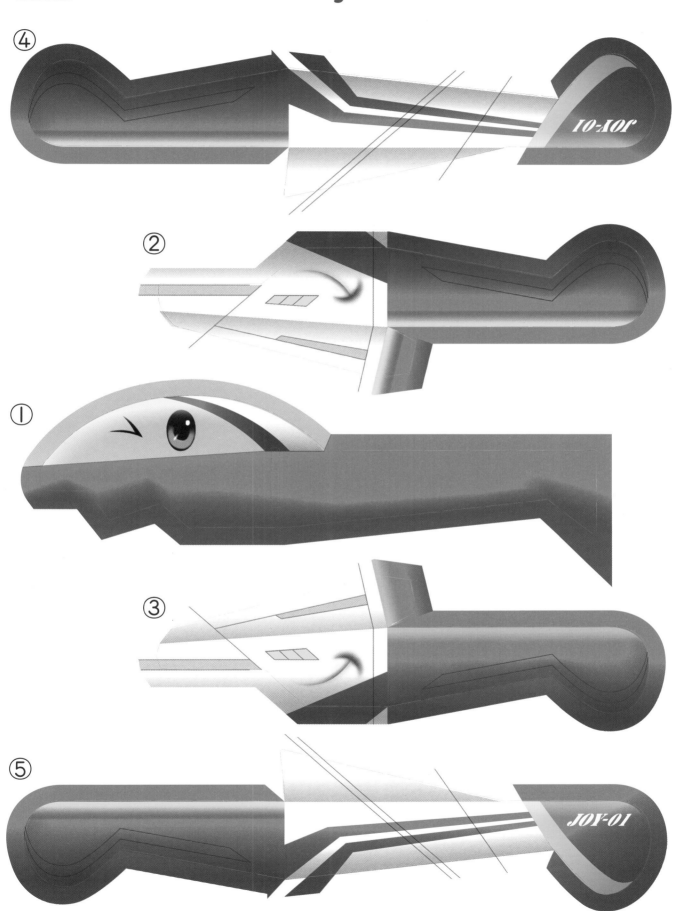

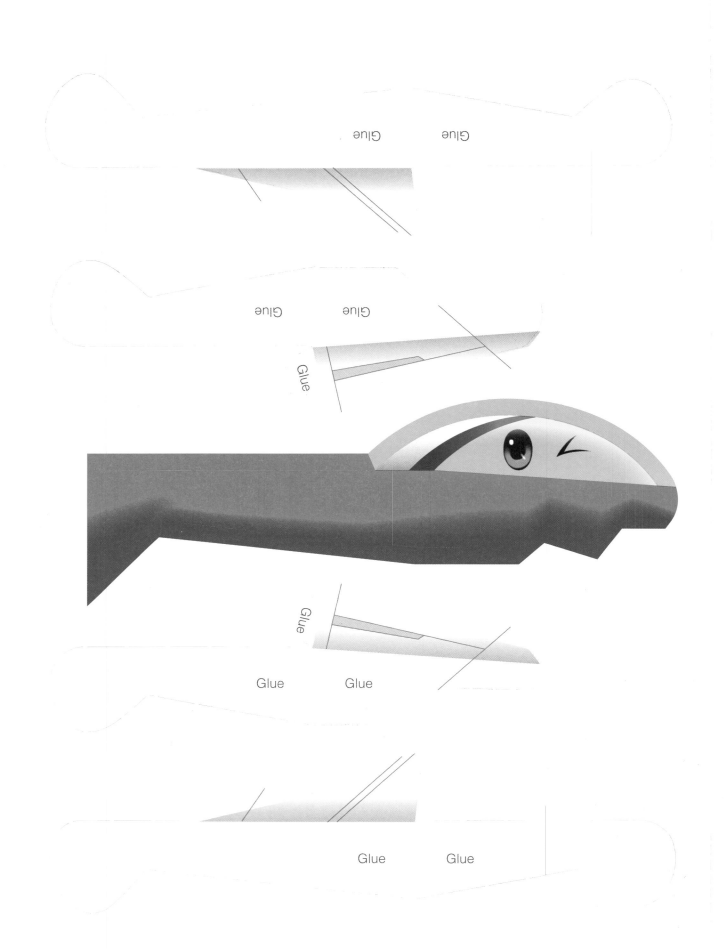

Glue    Glue

Glue    Glue

Glue

Glue

Glue    Glue

Glue    Glue

118

# No. 9 VTOL Drone "Joy"

·Remove along the lines and assemble according to the guide on page 45.

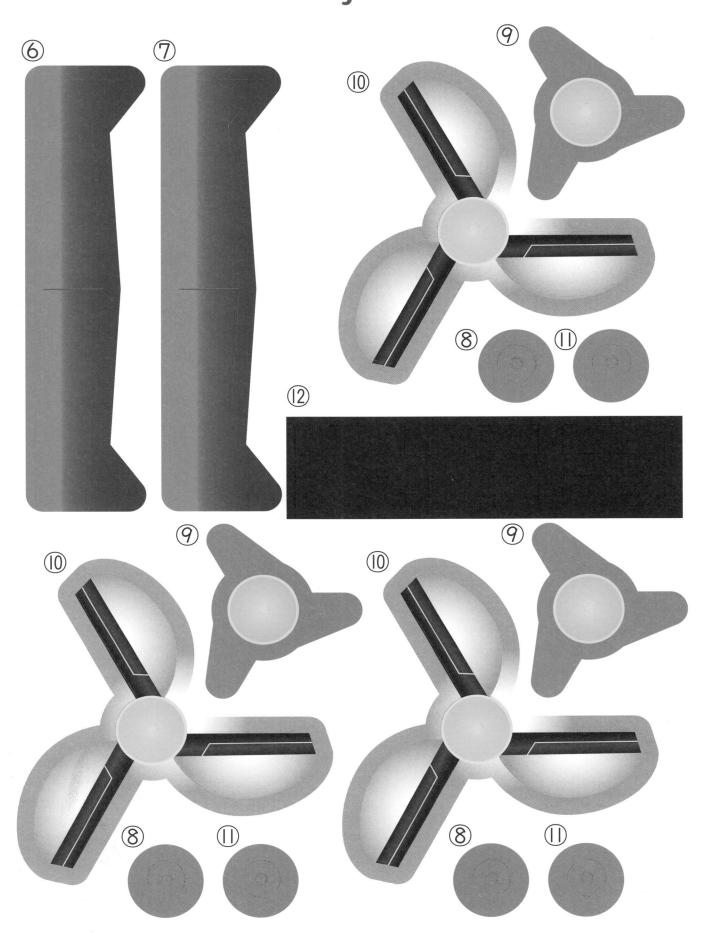

119

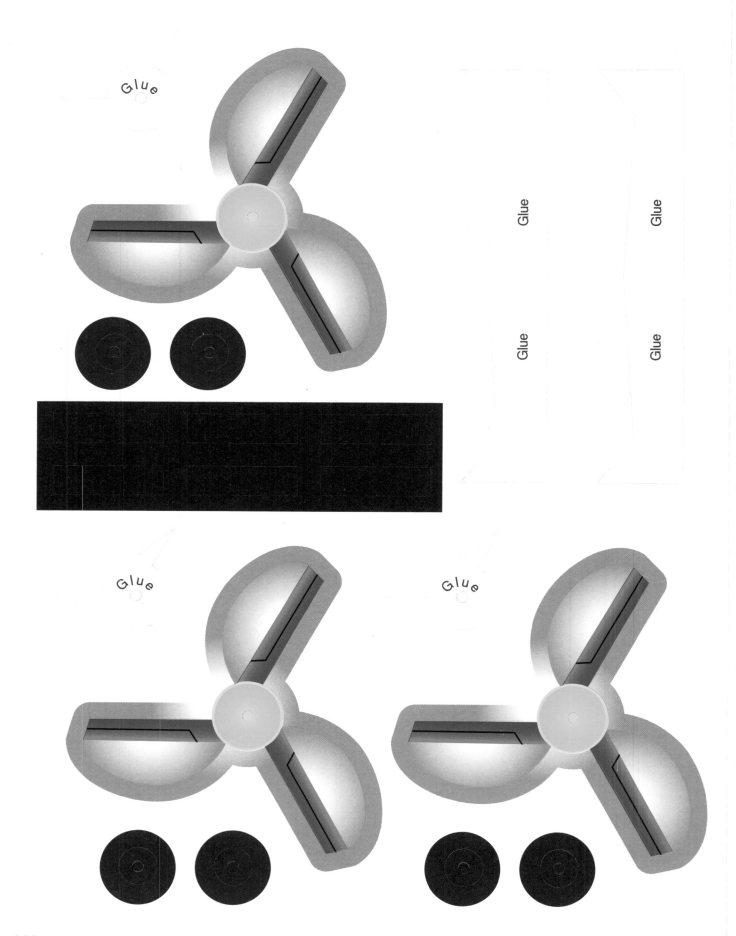

Glue

Glue

Glue

Glue

Glue

Glue

Glue

Glue